Arthur Conan Doyle

True Crime Collection - Real Murder Mysteries in 19th Century England
(Illustrated)

e-artnow 2020

Arthur Conan Doyle

True Crime Collection - Real Murder Mysteries in 19th Century England
(Illustrated)

Real Life Murders, Mysteries & Serial Killers of the Victorian Age

Illustrator: Sidney Paget

e-artnow, 2020
Contact: info@e-artnow.org

ISBN 978-80-273-3734-7

Contents

The Bravoes of Market-Drayton

To the north of the Wrekin, amid the rolling pastoral country which forms the borders of the counties of Shropshire and Staffordshire, there lies as fair a stretch of rustic England as could be found in the length and breadth of the land. Away to the south-east lie the great Staffordshire potteries; and farther south still, a long dusky pall marks the region of coal and of iron. On the banks of the Torn, however, there are sprinkled pretty country villages, and sleepy market towns which have altered little during the last hundred years, save that the mosses have grown longer, and the red bricks have faded into a more mellow tint. The traveller who in the days of our grandfathers was whirled through this beautiful region upon the box-seat of the Liverpool and Shrewsbury coach, was deeply impressed by the Arcadian simplicity of the peasants, and congratulated himself that innocence, long pushed out of the great cities, could still find a refuge amid these peaceful scenes. Most likely he would have smiled incredulously had he been informed that neither in the dens of Whitechapel nor in the slums of Birmingham was morality so lax or human life so cheap as in the fair region which he was admiring.

How such a state of things came about is difficult now to determine. It may be that the very quiet and beauty of the place caused those precautions and safeguards to be relaxed which may nip crime in the bud. Sir Robert Peel's new police had not yet been established. Even in London the inefficient "Charley" still reigned supreme, and was only replaced by the more efficient Bow Street "runner" after the crime had been committed. It may be imagined, therefore, that among the cider orchards and sheep-walks of Shropshire the arm of Justice, however powerful to revenge, could do little to protect. No doubt, small offenses undetected had led to larger ones, and those to larger still, until, in the year 1828, a large portion of the peasant population were banded together to defeat the law and to screen each other from the consequence of their misdeeds. This secret society might have succeeded in its object, had it not been for the unparalleled and most unnatural villainy of one of its members, whose absolutely callous and selfish conduct throws into the shade even the cold-blooded cruelty of his companions.

In the year 1827 a fine-looking young peasant named Thomas Ellson, in the prime of his manhood, was arrested at Market-Drayton upon two charges — the one of stealing potatoes, and the other of sheep-lifting, which in those days was still a hanging matter. The case for the prosecution broke down at the last moment on account of the inexplicable absence of an important witness named James Harrison. The crier of the court having three times summoned the absentee without any response, the charge was dismissed, and Thomas Ellson discharged with a caution. A louder crier still would have been needed to arouse James Harrison, for he was lying at that moment foully murdered in a hastily scooped grave within a mile of the court-house.

It appears that the gang which infested the country had, amidst their countless vices, one questionable virtue in their grim fidelity to each other. No red Macgregor attempting to free a clansman from the grasp of the Sassenach could have shown a more staunch and unscrupulous allegiance. The feeling was increased by the fact that the members of the league were generally connected with one another either by birth or marriage. When it became evident that Ellson's deliverance could only be wrought by the silencing of James Harrison, there appears to have been no hesitation as to the course to be followed.

The prime movers in the business were Ann Harris, who was the mother of Ellson by a former husband; and John Cox, his father-in-law. The latter was a fierce and turbulent old man, with two grown-up sons as savage as himself; while Mrs. Harris is described as being a ruddy-faced pleasant country woman, remarkable only for the brightness of her eyes. This pair of worthies having put their heads together, decided that James Harrison should be poisoned and that arsenic should be the drug. They applied, therefore, at several chemists', but without success. It is a remarkable commentary upon the general morality of Market-Drayton at this period that on applying at the local shop and being asked why she wanted arsenic, Mrs. Harris ingenuously answered that it was simply "to poison that scoundrel, James Harrison." The drug was refused; but the speech appears to have been passed by as a very ordinary one, for no steps were taken to inform the authorities or to warn the threatened man.

Being unable to effect their purpose in this manner, the mother and the father-in-law determined to resort to violence. Being old and feeble themselves, they resolved to hire assassins for the job, which appears to have been neither a difficult nor an expensive matter in those regions. For five pounds, three stout young men were procured who were prepared to deal in human lives as readily as any Italian bravo who ever handled a stiletto. Two of these were the sons of old Cox, John and Robert. The third was a young fellow named Pugh, who lodged in the same house as the proposed victim. The spectacle of three smock-frocked English yokels selling themselves at thirty-three shillings and fourpence a head to murder a man against whom they had no personal grudge is one which is happily unique in the annals of crime.

The men earned their blood-money. On the next evening, Pugh proposed to the unsuspecting Harrison that they should slip out together and steal bacon, an invitation which appears to have had a fatal seduction to the Draytonian of the period. Harrison accompanied him upon the expedition, and presently, in a lonely corner, they came upon the two Coxes. One of them was digging in a ditch. Harrison expressed some curiosity as to what work he could have on hand at that time of night. He little dreamed that it was his own grave upon which he was looking. Presently, Pugh seized him by the throat, John Cox tripped up his heels, and together they strangled him. They bundled the body into the hole, covered it carefully up, and calmly returned to their beds. Next morning, as already recorded, the court crier cried in vain, and Thomas Ellson became a free man once more.

Upon his liberation, his associates naturally enough explained to him with some exultation the means which they had adopted to silence the witness for the prosecution. The young Coxes, Pugh, and his mother all told him the same story. The unfortunate Mrs. Harris had already found occasion to regret the steps which she had taken, for Pugh, who appears to have been a most hardened young scoundrel, had already begun to extort money out of her on the strength of his knowledge. Robert Cox, too, had remarked to her with an oath: "If thee doesn't give me more money, I will fetch him and rear him up against thy door." The rustic villains seem to have seen their way to unlimited beer by working upon the feelings of the old country woman. One would think that the lowest depths of human infamy had been already plumbed in this matter; but it remained for Thomas Ellson, the rescued man, to cap all the iniquities of his companions. About a year after his release, he was apprehended upon a charge of fowl-stealing, and in order to escape the trifling punishment allotted to that offense, he instantly told the whole story of the doing away with James Harrison. Had his confession come from horror at their crime, it might have been laudable; but the whole circumstances of the case showed that it was merely a cold-blooded bid for the remission of a small sentence at the cost of the lives of his own mother and his associates. Deep as their guilt was, it had at least been incurred in order to save this heartless villain from the fate which he had well deserved.

The trial which ensued excited the utmost interest in all parts of England. Ann Harris, John Cox the younger, Robert Cox, and James Pugh were all arraigned for the murder of James Harrison. The wretched remnant of mortality had been dug up from the ditch, and could only be recognized by the clothes and by the colour of the hair. The whole case against the accused rested upon the very flimsiest evidence, save for Thomas Ellson's statement, which was delivered with a clearness and precision which no cross-examination could shake. He recounted the various conversations in which the different prisoners, including his mother, had admitted their guilt, as calmly and as imperturbably as though there were nothing at stake upon it. From the time when Pugh "'ticed un out o' feyther's house to steal some bacon," to the final tragedy, when he "gripped un by the throat," every detail came out in its due order. He met his mother's gaze steadily as he swore that she had confided to him that she had contributed fifty shillings towards the removing of the witness. No more repulsive spectacle has ever been witnessed in an English court of justice than this cold-blooded villain calmly swearing away the life of the woman who bore him, whose crime had arisen from her extravagant affection for him, and all to save himself from a temporary inconvenience.

Mr. Phillips, the counsel for the defense, did all that he could to shake Ellson's evidence; but though he aroused the loathing of the whole court by the skillful way in which he brought out the scoundrel's motives and character, he was unable to shake him as to his facts. A verdict of guilty was returned against the whole band, and sentence of death duly passed upon them.

On the 4th of July 1828 the awful punishment was actually carried out upon Pugh and the younger Cox, the two who had laid hands upon the deceased. Pugh declared that death was a relief to him, as Harrison was always, night and day, by his side. Cox, on the other hand, died sullenly, without any sign of repentance for the terrible crime for which his life was forfeited. Thomas Ellson was compelled to be present at the execution, as a warning to him to discontinue his evil practices.

Mrs. Harris and the elder Cox were carried across the seas, and passed the short remainder of their lives in the dreary convict barracks which stood upon the site of what is now the beautiful town of Sydney. The air of the Shropshire downs was the sweeter for the dispersal of the precious band; and it is on record that this salutary example brought it home to the rustics that the law was still a power in the land, and that, looking upon it as a mere commercial transaction, the trade of the bravo was not one which could flourish upon English soil.

The Holocaust of Manor Place

In the study of criminal psychology one is forced to the conclusion that the most dangerous of all types of mind is that of the inordinately selfish man. He is a man who has lost his sense of proportion. His own will and his own interest have blotted out for him the duty which he owes to the community. Impulsiveness, jealousy, vindictiveness are the fruitful parents of crime, but the insanity of selfishness is the most dangerous and also the most unlovely of them all. Sir Willoughby Patterne, the eternal type of all egoists, may be an amusing and harmless character as long as things go well with him, but let him be thwarted, let the thing which he desires be withheld from him, and the most monstrous results may follow. Huxley has said that a man in this life is for ever playing a game with an unseen opponent, who only makes his presence felt by exacting a penalty every time one makes a mistake in the game. The player who makes the mistake of selfishness may have a terrible forfeit to pay, but the unaccountable thing in the rules is that some, who are only spectators of his game, may have to help him in the paying. Read the Story of William Godfrey Youngman, and see how difficult it is to understand the rules under which these penalties are exacted. Learn also from it that selfishness is no harmless peccadillo, but that it is an evil root from which the most monstrous growths may spring.

About forty miles to the south of London, and close to the rather passé watering-place of Tunbridge Wells, there lies the little townlet of Wadhurst. It is situated within the borders of Sussex at a point which is close to the confines of Kent. The country is a rich pastoral one and the farmers are a flourishing race, for they are near enough to the Metropolis to take advantage of its mighty appetite. Among these farmers there lived in the year 1860 one Streeter, the master of a small homestead and the father of a fair daughter, Mary Wells Streeter. Mary was a strong, robust girl, some twenty years of age, skilled in all country work, and with some knowledge also of the town, for she had friends up there, and above all she had one friend, a young man of twenty-five, whom she had met upon one of her occasional visits, and who had admired her so that he had actually come down to Wadhurst after her, and had spent a night under her father's roof. The father had expressed no disapprobation of the suitor, a brisk, masterful young fellow, a little vague in his description of his own occupation and prospects, but an excellent fireside companion. And so it came about that the deep, town-bred William Godfrey Youngman became engaged to the simple, country-bred Mary Wells Streeter, William knowing all about Mary, but Mary very little about William.

The bundle of love-letters upon her lap.

July the 29th of that year fell upon a Sunday, and Mary sat in the afternoon in the window of the farm-house parlour, with her bundle of love- letters upon her lap, reading them again and yet again. Outside was the little square of green lawn, fringed with the homely luxuriance of an English country garden, the high hollyhocks, the huge nodding sunflowers, the bushes of fuchsia, and the fragrant clumps of sweet William. Through the open lattice came the faint, delicate scent of the lilac and the long, low droning of the bees. The farmer had lain down to the plethoric sleep of the Sunday afternoon, and Mary had the room to herself. There were fifteen love-letters in all some shorter, some longer, some wholly delightful, some with scattered business allusions, which made her wrinkle her pretty brows. There was this matter of the insurance, for example, which had cost her lover so much anxiety until she had settled it. No doubt he knew more of the world than she, but still it was strange that she, so young and so hale, should be asked and again asked to prepare herself for death. Even in the flush of her love those scattered words struck a chill to her heart. 'Dearest girl,' he had written, 'I have filled up the paper now, and took it to the life insurance office, and they will write to Mrs. James Boric today to get an answer on Saturday. So you can go to the office with me before two o'clock on Monday.' And then again, only two days later, he had begun his letter: 'You promised me faithfully over and over again, and I expect you to keep your promise, that you would be mine, and that your friends would not know it until we were married; but now, dearest Mary, if you will only let Mrs. James Bone write to the insurance office at once and go with me to have your life insured on Monday morning next!' So ran the extracts from the letters, and they perplexed Mary as she read them. But it was all over now, and he should mingle business no longer with his love, for she had yielded to his whim, and the insurance for £100 had been duly effected. It had cost her a quarterly payment of 10s. 4d., but it had seemed to please him, and so she would think of it no more.

There was a click of the garden-gate, and looking up she saw the porter from the station coming up the path with a note in his hand. Seeing her at the window he handed it in and departed, slyly smiling, a curious messenger of Cupid in his corduroys and clumping boots —a messenger of a grimmer god than Cupid, had he but known it. She had eagerly torn it open, and this was the message that she read:

'16, Manor Place, Newington, S.E. Saturday night, July 28th.

'My BELOVED POLLY,

'I have posted one letter to you this afternoon, but I find that I shall not have to go to Brighton tomorrow as I have had a letter from there with what I wanted inside of it, so, my dear girl, I have quite settled my business now and I am quite ready to see you now, therefore I send this letter to you. I will send this to London Bridge Station tomorrow morning by 6:30 o'clock and get the guard to take it to Wadhurst Station, to give it to the porter there, who will take it to your place. I can only give the guard something, so you can give the man who brings this a small sum. I shall expect to see you, my dear girl, on Monday morning by the first train. I will await your coming at London Bridge Station. I know the time the train arrives —a quarter to ten o'clock. I have promised to go to my uncle's tomorrow, so I cannot come down; but I will go with you home on Monday night or first thing Tuesday morning, and so return here again Tuesday night, to be ready to go anywhere on Wednesday; but you know all that I have told you, and I now expect that you will come up on Monday morning, when I shall be able to manage things as I expect to do. Excuse more now, my dearest Mary. I shall now go to bed to be up early tomorrow to take this letter. Bring or burn all your letters, my dear girl. Do not forget; and with kind love and respects to all I now sum up, awaiting to see you Monday morning a quarter to ten o'clock.

Believe me, ever your loving, affectionate,

WILLIAM GODFREY YOUNGMAN.'

A very pressing invitation this to a merry day in town; but there were certainly some curious phrases in it. What did he mean by saying that he would manage things as he expected to do? And why should she burn or bring her love-letters? There, at least, she was determined to disobey this masterful suitor who always 'expected' in so authoritative a fashion that she would do this or that. Her letters were much too precious to be disposed of in this off-hand fashion. She packed them back, sixteen of them now, into the little tin box in which she kept her simple treasures, and then ran to meet her father, whose step she heard upon the stairs, to tell him of her invitation and the treat which awaited her to-morrow.

At a quarter to ten next morning William Godfrey Youngman was waiting upon the platform of London Bridge Station to meet the Wadhurst train which was bringing his sweetheart up to town. No observer glancing down the straggling line of loiterers would have picked him out as the man whose name and odious fame would before another day was passed be household words to all the three million dwellers in London. In person he was of a goodly height and build, but commonplace in his appearance, and with a character which was only saved from insignificance through the colossal selfishness, tainted with insanity, which made him conceive that all things should bend before his needs and will. So distorted was his outlook that it even seemed to him that if he wished people to be deceived they must be deceived, and that the weakest device or excuse, if it came from him, would pass unquestioned. He had been a journeyman tailor, as his father was before him, but aspiring beyond this, he had sought and obtained a situation as footman to Dr. Duncan, of Covent Garden. Here he had served with credit for some time, but had finally resigned his post and had returned to his father's house, where for some time he had been living upon the hospitality of his hard-worked parents. He had talked vaguely of going into farming, and it was doubtless his short experience of Wadhurst with its sweet-smelling kine and Sussex breezes which had put the notion into his Cockney head.

They walked down the platform together.

But now the train rolls in, and there at a third-class window is Mary Streeter with her pink country cheeks, the pinker at the sight of her waiting lover. He takes her bag and they walk down the platform together amongst the crinolined women and baggy-trousered men whose pictures make the London of this date more strange to us than that of last century. He lives at Walworth, in South London, and a straw-strewn omnibus outside the station conveys them almost to the door. It was eleven o'clock when they arrived at Manor Place, where Youngman's family resided.

The household arrangements at Manor Place were peculiar. The architect having not yet evolved the flat in England, the people had attained the same result in another fashion. The tenant of a two-storied house resided upon the ground-floor, and then sub-let his first and second floors to other families. Thus, in the present instance, Mr. James Bevan occupied the ground, Mr. and Mrs. Beard the first, and the Youngman family the second, of the various floors of No. 16. Manor Place. The ceilings were thin and the stairs were in common, so it may be imagined that each family took a lively interest in the doings of its neighbour. Thus Mr. and Mrs. Beard of the first floor were well aware that young Youngman had brought his sweetheart home, and were even able through half-closed doors to catch a glimpse of her, and to report that his manner towards her was affectionate.

It was not a very large family to which he introduced her. The father departed to his tailoring at five o'clock every morning and returned at ten at night. There remained only the mother, a kindly, anxious, hard-working woman, and two younger sons aged eleven and seven. At eleven o'clock the boys were at school and the mother alone.She welcomed her country visitor, eyeing her meanwhile and summing her up as a mother would do when first she met the woman whom her son was likely to marry. They dined together, and then the two set forth to see something of the sights of London.

No record has been left of what the amusements were to which this singular couple turned: he with a savage, unrelenting purpose in his heart; she wondering at his abstracted manner, and chattering country gossip with the shadow of death already gathering thickly over her. One little incident has survived. One Edward Spicer, a bluff, outspoken publican who kept the Green Dragon in Bermondsey Street, knew Mary Streeter and her father. The couple called together at the inn, and Mary presented her lover. We have no means of knowing what repellent look mine host may have observed in the young man's face, or what malign trait he may have detected in his character, but he drew the girl aside and whispered that it was better for her to take a rope and hang herself in his skittle-alley than to marry such a man as that —a warning which seems to have met the same fate as most other warnings received by maidens of their lovers. In the evening they went to the theatre together to see one of Macready's tragedies.

She sat in the crowded pit
with her silent lover at her side.

How could she know as she sat in the crowded pit, with her silent lover at her side, that her own tragedy was far grimmer than any upon the stage? It was eleven o'clock before they were back once more at Manor Place.

The hard-working tailor had now returned, and the household all supped together. Then they had to be divided for the night between the two bedrooms, which were all the family possessed. The mother, Mary, and the boy of seven occupied the front one. The father slept on his own board in the back one, and in a bed beside him lay the young man and the boy of eleven. So they settled down to sleep as commonplace a family as any in London, with little thought that within a day the attention of all the great city would be centred upon those two dingy rooms and upon the fates of their inmates.

The father woke in the very early hours, and saw in the dim light of the dawn the tall figure of his son standing in white beside his bed. To some sleepy remark that he was stirring early the youth muttered an excuse and lay down once more. At five the tailor rose to his endless task, and at twenty minutes past he went down the stair and closed the hall door behind him. So passed away the only witness, and all that remains is conjecture and circumstantial evidence. No one will ever know the exact details of what occurred, and for the purpose of the chronicler it is as well, for such details will not bear to be too critically examined. The motives and mind of the murderer are of perennial interest to every student of human nature, but the vile record of his actual brutality may be allowed to pass away when the ends of justice have once been served by their recital.

I have said that on the floor under the Youngman's there lived a couple named Beard. At half-past five, a little after the time when the tailor had closed the hall door behind him, Mrs. Beard was disturbed by a sound which she took to be from children running up and down and playing. There was a light patter of feet on the floor above. But as she listened it struck her that there was something unusual in this romping at so early an hour, so she nudged her husband and asked him for his opinion. Then, as the two sat up in bed, straining their ears, there came from above them a gasping cry and the dull, soft thud of a falling body. Beard sprang out of bed and rushed upstairs until his head came upon the level of the Youngman's landing. He saw enough to send him shrieking down to Mr. Bevan upon the ground-floor. 'For God's sake, come here! There is murder!' he roared, fumbling with his shaking fingers at the handle of the landlord's bedroom.

His summons did not find the landlord entirely unprepared. That ill-boding thud had been loud enough to reach his ears. He sprang palpitating from his bed, and the two men in their nightdresses ascended the creaking staircase, their frightened faces lit up by the blaze of golden sunlight of a July morning. Again they do not seem to have got farther than the point from which they could see the landing. That confused huddle of white-clad figures littered over the passage, with those glaring smears and blotches, were more than their nerves could stand. They could count three lying there, stark dead upon the landing. And there was someone moving in the bedroom. It was coming towards them. With horror-dilated eyes they saw William Godfrey Youngman framed in the open doorway, his white nightdress brilliant with ghastly streaks and the sleeve hanging torn over his hand.

'Mr. Beard,' he cried, when he saw the two bloodless faces upon the stairs, 'for God's sake fetch a surgeon! I believe there is some alive yet!' Then, as they turned and ran down stairs again, he called after them the singular explanation to which he ever afterwards adhered. 'My mother has done all this,' he cried; 'she murdered my two brothers and my sweetheart, and I in self-defence believe that I have murdered her.'

The two men did not stop to discuss the question with him. They had both rushed to their rooms and huddled on some clothes Then they ran out of the house in search of a surgeon and a policeman, leaving Youngman still standing on the stair repeating his strange explanation. How sweet the morning air must have seemed to them when they were once clear of the accursed house, and how the honest milkmen, with their swinging tins, must have stared at those two rushing and dishevelled figures. But they had not far to go. John Varney, of P Division, as solid and unimaginative as the law which he represents, was standing at the street corner, and he came clumping back with reassuring slowness and dignity.

'Oh, policeman, here is a sight! What shall I do?' cried Youngman, as he saw the glazed official hat coming up the stair.

Constable Varney is not shaken by that horrid cluster of death. His advice is practical and to the point.

'Go and dress yourself!' said he.

'I struck my mother; but it was in self defence,' cried the other. 'Would you not have done the same? It is the law.'

Constable Varney is not to be drawn into giving a legal opinion, but he is quite convinced that the best thing for Youngman to do is to put on some clothes.

And now a crowd had begun to assemble in the street, and another policeman and an inspector had arrived. It was clear that, whether Youngman's story was correct or not, he was a self-confessed homicide, and that the law must hold her grip of him. But when a dagger-shaped knife, splintered by the force of repeated blows, was found upon the floor, and Youngman had to confess that it belonged to him; when also it was observed that ferocious strength and energy were needed to produce the wounds inflicted, it became increasingly evident that, instead of being a mere victim of circumstances, this man was one of the criminals of a century. But all evidence must be circumstantial, for mother, sweetheart, brothers-the mouths of all were closed in the one indiscriminate butchery.

The horror and the apparent purposelessness of the deed roused public excitement and indignation to the highest pitch. The miserable sum for which poor Mary was insured appeared to be the sole motive of the crime; the prisoner's eagerness to have the business concluded, and his desire to have the letters destroyed in which he had urged it, forming the strongest evidence against him. At the same time, his calm assumption that things would be arranged as he wished them to be, and that the Argus Insurance Office would pay over the money to one who was neither husband nor relative of the deceased, pointed to an ignorance of the ways of business or a belief in his own powers of managing, which in either case resembled insanity. When in addition it came out at the trial that the family was sodden with lunacy upon both sides, that the wife's mother and the husband's brother were in asylums, and that the husband's father had been in an asylum, but had become 'tolerably sensible' before his death, it is doubtful whether the case should not have been judged upon medical rather than upon criminal grounds. In these more scientific and more humanitarian days it is perhaps doubtful whether Youngman would have been hanged, but there was never any doubt as to his fate in 1860.

The trial came off at the Central Criminal Court upon August 16th before Mr. Justice Williams. Few fresh details came out, save that the knife had been in prisoner's possession for some time. He had exhibited it once in a bar, upon which a bystander, with the good British love of law and order, had remarked that that was not a fit knife for any man to carry.

'Anybody,' said Youngman, in reply, 'has the right to carry such a knife if he thinks proper in his own defence.'

Perhaps the objector did not realize how near he may have been at that moment to getting its point between his ribs. Nothing serious against the prisoner's previous character came out at the trial, and he adhered steadfastly to his own account of the tragedy. In summing up, however, Justice Williams pointed out that if the prisoner's story were true it meant that he had disarmed his mother and got possession of the knife. What necessity was there, then, for him to kill her? and why should he deal her repeated wounds? This argument, and the fact that there were no stains upon the hands of the mother, prevailed with the jury, and sentence was duly passed upon the prisoner.

Youngman had shown an unmoved demeanour in the dock, but he gave signs of an irritable, and occasionally of a violent, temper in prison. His father visited him, and the prisoner burst instantly into fierce reproaches against his treatment of his family-reproaches for which there seem to have been no justification. Another thing which appeared to have galled him to the quick was the remark of the publican, which first reached his ears at the trial, to the effect that Mary had better hang herself in the skittle-yard than marry such a man. His self-esteem, the strongest trait in his nature, was cruelly wounded by such a speech.

His father visited him.

'Only one thing I wish,' he cried, furiously, 'that I could get hold of this man Spicer, for I would strike his head off.' The unnatural and bloodthirsty character of the threat is characteristic of the homicidal maniac. 'Do you suppose,' he added, with a fine touch of vanity, 'that a man of my determination and spirit would have heard these words used in my presence without striking the man who used them to the ground?'

But in spite of exhortation and persuasion he carried his secret with him to the grave. He never varied from the story which he had probably concocted before the event.

'Do not leave the world with a lie on your lips.' said the chaplain, as they walked to the scaffold.

'Well, if I wanted to tell a lie I would say that I did it.' was his retort. He hoped to the end with his serene self-belief that the story which he had put forward could not fail eventually to be accepted. Even on the scaffold he was on the alert for a reprieve.

It was on the 4th of September, a little more than a month after the commission of his crime, that he was led out in front of Horsemonger Gaol to suffer his punishment. A concourse of

30,000 people, many of whom had waited all night, raised a brutal howl at his appearance. It was remarked at the time that it was one of the very few instances of capital punishment in which no sympathizer or philanthropist of any sort could be found to raise a single voice against the death penalty. The man died quietly and coolly.

'Thank you, Mr. Jessopp,' said he to the chaplain, 'for your great kindness. See my brother and take my love to him, and all at home.'

And so, with the snick of a bolt and the jar of a rope, ended one of the most sanguinary, and also one of the most unaccountable, incidents in English criminal annals. That the man was guilty seems to admit no doubt, and yet it must be confessed that circumstantial evidence can never be absolutely convincing, and that it is only the critical student of such cases who realizes how often a damning chain of evidence may, by some slight change, be made to bear an entirely different interpretation.

The Love Affair of George Vincent Parker

The student of criminal annals will find upon classifying his cases that the two causes which are the most likely to incite a human being to the crime of murder are the lust of money and the black resentment of a disappointed love. Of these the latter are both rarer and more interesting, for they are subtler in their inception and deeper in their psychology. The mind can find no possible sympathy with the brutal greed and selfishness which weighs a purse against a life; but there is something more spiritual in the case of the man who is driven by jealousy and misery to a temporary madness of violence. To use the language of science it is the passionate as distinguished from the instinctive criminal type. The two classes of crime may be punished by the same severity, but we feel that they are not equally sordid, and that none of us is capable of saying how he might act if his affections and his self-respect were suddenly and cruelly outraged. Even when we indorse the verdict it is still possible to feel some shred of pity for the criminal. His offence has not been the result of a self-interested and cold-blooded plotting, but it has been the consequence-however monstrous and disproportionate-of a cause for which others were responsible. As an example of such a crime I would recite the circumstances connected with George Vincent Parker, making some alteration in the names of persons and of places wherever there is a possibility that pain might be inflicted by their disclosure.

Nearly forty years ago there lived in one of our Midland cities a certain Mr. Parker, who did a considerable business as a commission agent. He was an excellent man of affairs, and during those progressive years which intervened between the Crimean and the American wars his fortune increased rapidly.

He built himself a villa in a pleasant suburb outside the town, and being blessed with a charming and sympathetic wife there was every prospect that the evening of his days would be spent in happiness. The only trouble which he had to contend with was his inability to understand the character of his only son, or to determine what plans he should make for his future.

George Vincent Parker, the young man in question, was of a type which continually recurs and which verges always upon the tragic. By some trick of atavism he had no love for the great city and its roaring life, none for the weary round of business, and no ambition to share the rewards which successful business brings. He had no sympathy with his father's works or his father's ways, and the life of the office was hateful to him. This aversion to work could not, however, be ascribed to viciousness or indolence. It was innate and constitutional. In other directions his mind was alert and receptive. He loved music and showed a remarkable aptitude for it. He was an excellent linguist and had some taste in painting. In a word, he was a man of artistic temperament, with all the failings of nerve and of character which that temperament implies. In London he would have met hundreds of the same type, and would have found a congenial occupation in making small incursions into literature and dabbling in criticism. Among the cotton-brokers of the Midlands his position was at that time an isolated one, and his father could only shake his head and pronounce him to be quite unfit to carry on the family business. He was gentle in his disposition, reserved with strangers, but very popular among his few friends. Once or twice it had been remarked that he was capable of considerable bursts of passion when he thought himself ill-used.

This is a type of man for whom the practical workers of the world have no affection, but it is one which invariably appeals to the feminine nature. There is a certain helplessness about it and a naive appeal for sympathy to which a woman's heart readily responds-and it is the strongest, most vigorous woman who is the first to answer the appeal.

*It was at a musical evening at the house of
a local doctor that he first met Miss Groves.*

We do not know what other consolers this quiet dilettante may have found, but the details of one such connection have come down to us. It was at a musical evening at the house of a local doctor that he first met Miss Mary Groves. The doctor was her uncle, and she had come to town to visit him, but her life was spent in attendance upon her grandfather, who was a very virile old gentleman, whose eighty years did not prevent him from fulfilling all the duties of a country gentleman, including those of the magisterial bench.

After the quiet of a secluded manor-house the girl in the first flush of her youth and her beauty enjoyed the life of the town, and seems to have been particularly attracted by this refined young musician, whose appearance and manners suggested that touch of romance for which a young girl craves. He on his side was drawn to her by her country freshness and by the sympathy which she showed for him. Before she returned to the Manor-house friendship had grown into love and the pair were engaged.

But the engagement was not looked upon with much favour by either of the families concerned. Old Parker had died, and his widow was left with sufficient means to live in comfort, but it became more imperative than ever that some profession should be found for the son. His invincible repugnance to business still stood in the way. On the other hand the young lady came of a good stock, and her relations, headed by the old country squire, objected to her marriage with a penniless young man of curious tastes and character. So for four years the engagement dragged along, during which the lovers corresponded continually, but seldom met. At the end of that time he was twenty-five and she was twenty-three, but the prospect of their union seemed as remote as ever. At last the prayers of her relatives overcame her constancy, and she took steps to break the tie which held them together. This she endeavoured to do by a change in the tone of her letters, and by ominous passages to prepare him for the coming blow.

On August 12th, 18 — she wrote that she had met a clergyman who was the most delightful man she had ever seen in her life. 'He has been staying with us,' she said, 'and grandfather thought that he would just suit me, but that would not do.' This passage, in spite of the few lukewarm words of reassurance, disturbed young Vincent Parker exceedingly. His mother testified afterwards to the extreme depression into which he was thrown, which was the less remarkable as he was a man who suffered from constitutional low spirits, and who always took the darkest view upon every subject. Another letter reached him next day which was more decided in its tone.

'I have a good deal to say to you, and it had better be said at once,' said she. 'My grandfather has found out about our correspondence, and is wild that there should be any obstacle to the match between the clergyman and me. I want you to release me that I may have it to say that I am free. Don't take this too hardly, in pity for me. I shall not marry if I can help it.'

This second letter had an overpowering effect. His state was such that his mother had to ask a family friend to sit up with him all night. He paced up and down in an extreme state of nervous excitement, bursting constantly into tears. When he lay down his hands and feet twitched convulsively. Morphia was administered, but without effect. He refused all food. He had the utmost difficulty in answering the letter, and when he did so next day it was with the help of the friend who had stayed with him all night. His answer was reasonable and also affectionate.

'My dearest Mary,' he said. 'Dearest you will always be to me. To say that I am not terribly cut up would be a lie, but at any rate you know that I am not the man to stand in your way. I answer nothing to your last letter except that I wish to hear from your own lips what your wishes are, and I will then accede to them. You know me too well to think that I would then give way to any unnecessary nonsense or sentimentalism. Before I leave England I wish to see you once again, and for the last time, though God knows what misery it gives me to say so. You will admit that my desire to see you is but natural. Say in your next where you will meet me. Ever, dearest Mary, your affectionate GEORGE.'

Next, day he wrote another letter in which he again implored her to give him an appointment, saying that any place between their house and Standwell, the nearest village, would do. 'I am ill and thoroughly upset, and I do not wonder that you are,' said he. 'We shall both be happier and better in mind as well as in body after this last interview. I shall be at your appointment, *coûte qu'il coûte*. Always your affectionate GEORGE.'

There seems to have been an answer to this letter actually making an appointment, for he wrote again upon Wednesday, the 19th. 'My dear Mary,' said he, 'I will only say here that I will arrive by the train you mention and that I hope, dear Mary, that you will not bother yourself unnecessarily about all this so far as I am concerned. For my own peace of mind I wish to see you, which I hope you won't think selfish. *Du reste* I only repeat what I have already said. I have but to hear from you what your wishes are and they shall be complied with. I have sufficient *savoir faire* not to make a bother about what cannot be helped. Don't let me be the cause of any row between you and your grandpapa. If you like to call at the inn I will not stir out until you come, but I leave this to your judgment.'

As Professor Owen would reconstruct an entire animal out of a single bone, so from this one little letter the man stands flagrantly revealed. The scraps of French, the self-conscious allusion to his own *savoir faire*, the florid assurances which mean nothing, they are all so many strokes in a subtle self-portrait.

Miss Groves had already repented the appointment which she had given him. There may have been some traits in this eccentric lover whom she had abandoned which recurred to her memory and warned her not to trust herself in his power. —My dear George,' she wrote-and her letter must have crossed his last one —'I write this in the greatest haste to tell you not to come on any account. I leave here today, and can't tell when I can or shall be back. I do not wish to see you if it can possibly be avoided, and indeed there will be no chance now, so we had best end this state of suspense at once and say good-bye without seeing each other. I feel sure I could not stand the meeting. If you write once more within the next three days I shall get it, but not later than that time without its being seen, for my letters are strictly watched and even opened. Yours truly, MARY.'

He wandered about the coffee-room muttering to himself.

This letter seems to have brought any vague schemes which may have been already forming in the young man's mind to an immediate head. If he had only three days in which he might see her he could not afford to waste any time. On the same day he went to the county town, but as it was late he did not go on to Standwell, which was her station. The waiters at the Midland Hotel noticed his curious demeanour and his vacant eye. He wandered about the coffee-room muttering to himself, and although he ordered chops and tea he swallowed nothing but some brandy and soda. Next morning, August 21st, he took a ticket to Standwell and arrived there at half-past eleven. From Standwell Station to the Manor-house where Miss Groves resided with the old squire is two miles. There is an inn close to the station called "The Bull's Head." Vincent Parker called there and ordered some brandy. He then asked whether a note had been left for his, and seemed much disturbed upon hearing that there was none. Then, the time being about a quarter past twelve, he went off in the direction of the Manor-house.

About two miles upon the other side of the Manor-house, and four miles from the Bull's Head Inn, there is a thriving grammar school, the head master of which was a friend of the Groves family and had some slight acquaintance with Vincent Parker. The young man thought, therefore, that this would be the best place for him to apply for information, and he arrived at the school about half-past one. The head master was no doubt considerably astonished at the appearance of this dishevelled and brandy-smelling visitor, but he answered his questions with discretion and courtesy.

'I have called upon you,' said Parker, 'as a friend of Miss Groves. I suppose you know that there is an engagement between us?'

'I understood that there *was* an engagement, and that it had been broken off,' said the master.

'Yes,' Parker answered. 'she has written to me to break off the engagement and declines to see me. I want to know how matters stand.'

'Anything I may know,' said the master, 'is in confidence, and so I cannot tell you.'

'I will find it out sooner or later,' said Parker, and then asked who the clergyman was who had been staying at the Manor-house. The master acknowledged that there had been one, but refused to give the name. Parker then asked whether Miss Groves was at the Manor-house and if any coercion was being used to her. The other answered that she was at the Manor-house and that no coercion was being used.

'Sooner or later I must see her,' said Parker. 'I have written to release her from her engagement, but I must hear from her own lips that she gives me up. She is of age and must please herself. I know that I am not a good match, and I do not wish to stand in her way.'

The master then remarked that it was time for school, but that he should be free again at half-past four if Parker had anything more to say to him, and Parker left, promising to return. It is not known how he spent the next two hours, but he may have found some country inn in which he obtained some luncheon. At half-past four he was back at the school, and asked the master for advice as to how to act. The master suggested that his best course was to write a note to Miss Groves and to make an appointment with her for next morning.

'If you were to call at the house, perhaps Miss Groves would see you,' said this sympathetic and most injudicious master.

'I will do so and get it off my mind,' said Vincent Parker.

It was about five o'clock when he left the school, his manner at that time being perfectly calm and collected.

It was forty minutes later when the discarded lover arrived at the house of his sweetheart. He knocked at the door and asked for Miss. Groves. She had probably seen him as he came down the drive, for she met him at the drawing-room door as he came in, and she invited him to come with her into the garden. Her heart was in her mouth, no doubt, lest her grandfather should see him and a scene ensue. It was safer to have him in the garden than in the house. They walked out, therefore, and half an hour later they were seen chatting quietly upon one of the benches. A little afterwards the maid went out and told Miss Groves that tea was ready. She came in alone, and it is suggestive of the views taken by the grandfather that there seems to have been no question about Parker coming in also to tea. She came out again into the garden and sat for a long time with the young man, after which they seem to have set off together for a stroll down the country lanes. What passed during that walk, what recriminations upon his part, what retorts upon hers, will never now be known. They were only once seen in the course of it. At about half-past eight o'clock a labourer, coming up a long lane which led from the high road to the Manor-house, saw a man and a woman walking together. As he passed them he recognised in the dusk that the lady was Miss Groves, the granddaughter of the squire. When he looked back he saw that they had stopped and were standing face to face conversing.

"Take me home!" she whispered. "Take me home!"

A very short time after this Reuben Conway, a workman, was passing down this lane when he heard a low sound of moaning. He stood listening, and in the silence of the country evening he became aware that this ominous sound was drawing nearer to him. A wall flanked one side of the lane, and as he stared about him his eye caught something moving slowly down the black shadow at the side. For a moment it must have seemed to him to be some wounded animal, but as he approached it he saw to his astonishment that it was a woman who was slowly stumbling along, guiding and supporting herself by her hand against the wall. With a cry of horror he found himself looking into the face of Miss Groves, glimmering white through the darkness.

'Take me home!' she whispered. 'Take me home! The gentleman down there has been murdering me.'

The horrified labourer put his arms round her, and carried her for about twenty yards towards home.

'Can you see anyone down the lane?' she asked, when he stopped for breath.

He looked, and through the dark tunnel of trees he saw a black figure moving slowly behind them. The labourer waited, still propping up the girl's head, until young Parker overtook them.

'Who has been murdering Miss Groves?' asked Reuben Conway.

'I have stabbed her,' said Parker, with the utmost coolness.

'Well, then, you had best help me to carry her home,' said the labourer. So down the dark lane moved that singular procession: the rustic and the lover, with the body of the dying girl between them.

'Poor Mary!' Parker muttered. 'Poor Mary! You should not have proved false to me!'

When they got as far as the lodge-gate Parker suggested that Reuben Conway should run and get something which might stanch the bleeding. He went, leaving these tragic lovers together for the last time. When he returned he found Parker holding something to her throat.

'Is she living?' he asked.

'She is,' said Parker.

'Oh, take me home!' wailed the poor girl. A little farther upon their dolorous journey they met two farmers, who helped them.

'Who has done this?' asked one of them.

'He knows and I know,' said Parker, gloomily. 'I am the man who has done this, and I shall be hanged for it. I have done it, and there is no question about that at all.'

These replies never seem to have brought insult or invective upon his head, for everyone appears to have been silenced by the overwhelming tragedy of the situation.

'I am dying!' gasped poor Mary, and they were the last words which she ever said. Inside the hall-gates they met the poor old squire running wildly up on some vague rumour of a disaster. The bearers stopped as they saw the white hair gleaming through the darkness.

'What is amiss?' he cried.

Parker said, calmly, 'It is your grand-daughter Mary murdered.'

'Who did it?' shrieked the old man.

'I did it.'

'Who are you?' he cried.

'My name is Vincent Parker.'

'Why did you do it?'

'She has deceived me, and the woman who deceives me must die.'

The calm concentration of his manner seems to have silenced all reproaches.

'I told her I would kill her,' said he, as they all entered the house together. 'She knew my temper.'

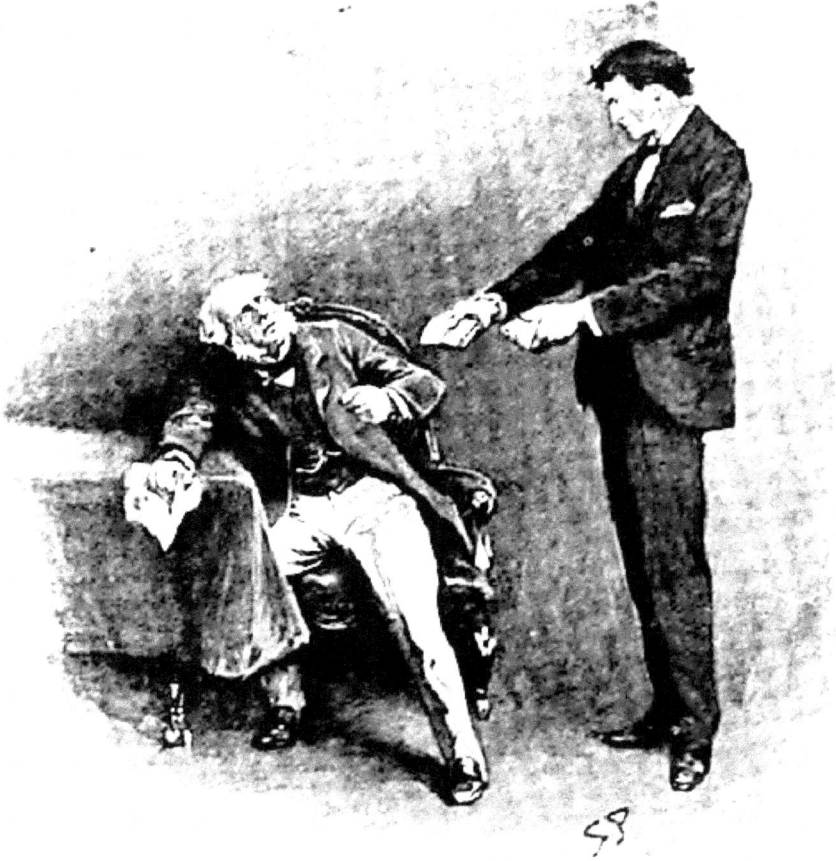

"Will you take care of these?" he said.

The body was carried into the kitchen and laid upon the table. In the meantime Parker had followed the bewildered and heart-broken old man into the drawing-room, and holding out a handful of things, including his watch and some money, he asked him if he would take care of them. The squire angrily refused. He then took two bundles of her letters out of his pocket — all that was left of their miserable love story.

'Will you take care of these?' said he. 'You may read them, burn them, do what you like with them. I don't wish them to be brought into court.'

The grandfather took the letters and they were duly burned.

And now the doctor and the policeman, the twin attendants upon violence, came hurrying down the avenue. Poor Mary was dead upon the kitchen table, with three great wounds upon her throat. How, with a severed carotid, she could have come so far or lived so long is one of the marvels of the case. As to the policeman, he had no trouble in looking for his prisoner. As he entered the room Parker walked towards him and said that he wished to give himself up for murdering a young lady. When asked if he were aware of the nature of the charge he said, 'Yes, quite so, and I will go with you quietly, only let me see her first.'

'What have you done with the knife?' asked the policeman.

Parker produced it from his pocket, a very ordinary one with a clasp blade. It is remarkable that two other penknives were afterwards found upon him. They took him into the kitchen and he looked at his victim.

'I am far happier now that I have done it than before, and I hope that she is.' said he.

This is the record of the murder of Mary Groves by Vincent Parker, a crime characterized by all that inconsequence and grim artlessness which distinguish fact from fiction. In fiction we make people say and do what we should conceive them to be likely to say or do, but in fact they say and do what no one would ever conceive to be likely. That those letters should be a prelude to a murder, or that after a murder the criminal should endeavour to stanch the wounds of his victim, or hold such a conversation as that described with the old squire, is what no human invention would hazard. One finds it very difficult on reading all the letters and weighing the facts to suppose that Vincent Parker came out that day with the preformed intention of killing his former sweetheart. But whether the dreadful idea was always there, or whether it came in some mad flash of passion provoked by their conversation, is what we shall never know. It is certain that she could not have seen anything dangerous in him up to the very instant of the crime, or she would certainly have appealed to the labourer who passed them in the lane.

His mother appeared in the witness-box.

The case, which excited the utmost interest through the length and breadth of England, was tried before Baron Martin at the next assizes. There was no need to prove the guilt of the prisoner, since he openly gloried in it, but the whole question turned upon his sanity, and led to some curious complications which have caused the whole law upon the point to be reformed. His relations were called to show that madness was rampant in the family, and that out of ten cousins five were insane. His mother appeared in the witness-box contending with dreadful vehemence that her son was mad, and that her own marriage had been objected to on the ground of the madness latent in her blood. All the witnesses agreed that the prisoner was not an ill-tempered man, but sensitive, gentle, and accomplished, with a tendency to melancholy. The prison chaplain affirmed that he had held conversations with Parker, and that his moral perception seemed to be so entirely wanting that he hardly knew right from wrong. Two specialists in lunacy examined him, and said that they were of opinion that he was of unsound mind. The opinion was based upon the fact that the prisoner declared that he could not see that he had done any wrong.

'Miss Groves was promised to me,' said he, 'and therefore she was mine. I could do what I liked with her. Nothing short of a miracle will alter my convictions.'

The doctor attempted to argue with him. 'Suppose anyone took a picture from you, what steps would you take to recover it?' he asked.

'I should demand restitution,' said he 'if not, I should take the thief's life without compunction.'

The doctor pointed out that the law was there to be appealed to, but Parker answered that he had been born into the world without being consulted, and therefore he recognised the right of no man to judge him. The doctor's conclusion was that his moral sense was more vitiated than any case that he had seen. That this constitutes madness would, however, be a dangerous doctrine to urge, since it means that if a man were only wicked enough he would be screened from the punishment of his wickedness.

Baron Martin summed up in a common-sense manner. He declared that the world was full of eccentric people, and that to grant them all the immunity of madness would be a public danger. To be mad within the meaning of the law a criminal should be in such a state as not to know that he has committed crime or incurred punishment. Now, it was clear that Parker did know this, since he had talked of being hanged. The Baron accordingly accepted the jury's finding of 'Guilty,' and sentenced the prisoner to death.

There the matter might very well have ended were it not for Baron Martin's conscientious scruples. His own ruling had been admirable, but the testimony of the mad doctors weighed heavily upon him, and his conscience was uneasy at the mere possibility that a man who was really not answerable for his actions should lose his life through his decision. It is probable that the thought kept him awake that night, for next morning he wrote to the Secretary of State, and told him that he shrank from the decision of such a case.

The Secretary of State, having carefully read the evidence and the judge's remarks, was about to confirm the decision of the latter, when, upon the very eve of the execution, there came a report from the gaol visitors — perfectly untrained observers-that Parker was showing undoubted signs of madness. This being so the Secretary of State had no choice but to postpone the execution, and to appoint a commission of four eminent alienists to report upon the condition of the prisoner. These four reported unanimously that he was perfectly sane. It is an unwritten law, however, that a prisoner once reprieved is never executed, so Vincent Parker's sentence was commuted to penal servitude for life —a decision which satisfied, upon the whole, the conscience of the public.

THE END

The Debatable Case of Mrs. Emsley

In the fierce popular indignation which is excited by a sanguinary crime there is a tendency, in which judges and juries share, to brush aside or to treat as irrelevant those doubts the benefit of which is supposed to be one of the privileges of the accused. Lord Tenterden has whittled down the theory of doubt by declaring that a jury is justified in giving its verdict upon such evidence as it would accept to be final in any of the issues of life. But when one looks back and remembers how often one has been very sure and yet has erred in the issues of life, how often what has seemed certain has failed us, and that which appeared impossible has come to pass, we feel that if the criminal law has been conducted upon such principles it is probably itself the giant murderer of England. Far wiser is the contention that it is better that ninety-nine guilty should escape than that one innocent man should suffer, and that, therefore, if it can be claimed that there is one chance in a hundred in favour of the prisoner he is entitled to his acquittal. It cannot be doubted that if the Scotch verdict of 'Not proven,' which neither condemns nor acquits, had been permissible in England it would have been the outcome of many a case which, under our sterner law, has ended upon the scaffold. Such a verdict would, I fancy, have been hailed as a welcome compromise by the judge and the jury who investigated the singular circumstances which attended the case of Mrs. Mary Emsley.

The stranger in London who wanders away from the beaten paths and strays into the quarters in which the workers dwell is astounded by their widespread monotony, by the endless rows of uniform brick houses broken only by the corner public-houses and more infrequent chapels which are scattered amongst them. The expansion of the great city has been largely caused by the covering of district after district with these long lines of humble dwellings, and the years between the end of the Crimean War and 1860 saw great activity in this direction. Many small builders by continually mortgaging what they had done, and using the capital thus acquired to start fresh works which were themselves in turn mortgaged, contrived to erect street after street, and eventually on account of the general rise of property to make considerable fortunes. Amongst these astute speculators there was one John Emsley, who, dying, left his numerous houses and various interests to his widow Mary.

Mrs. Mary Emsley.

Mary Emsley, now an old woman, had lived too long in a humble fashion to change her way of life. She was childless, and all the activities of her nature were centred upon the economical management of her property, and the collection of the weekly rents from the humble tenants who occupied them. A grim, stern, eccentric woman, she was an object of mingled dislike and curiosity among the inhabitants of Grove Road, Stepney, in which her house was situated. Her possessions extended over Stratford, Bow, and Bethnal Green, and in spite of her age she made long journeys, collecting, evicting, and managing, always showing a great capacity for the driving of a hard bargain. One of her small economies was that when she needed help in managing these widespread properties she preferred to employ irregular agents to engaging a salaried representative. There were many who did odd jobs for her, and among them were two men whose names were destined to become familiar to the public. The one was John Emms, a cobbler; the other George Mullins, a plasterer.

Mary Emsley, in spite of her wealth, lived entirely alone, save that on Saturdays a charwoman called to clean up the house. She showed also that extreme timidity and caution which are often characteristic of those who afterwards perish by violence-as if there lies in human nature some vague instinctive power of prophecy. It was with reluctance that she ever opened her door, and each visitor who approached her was reconnoitred from the window of her area. Her fortune would have permitted her to indulge herself with every luxury, but the house was a small one, consisting of two stories and a basement, with a neglected back garden, and her mode of life was even simpler than her dwelling. It was a singular and most unnatural old age.

Mrs. Emsley was last seen alive upon the evening of Monday, August 13th, 1860. Upon that date, at seven o'clock, two neighbours perceived her sitting at her bedroom window. Next morning, shortly after ten, one of her irregular retainers called upon some matter of brass taps, but was unable to get any answer to his repeated knockings. During that Tuesday many visitors had the same experience, and the Wednesday and Thursday passed without any sign of life within the house. One would have thought that this would have aroused instant suspicions, but the neighbours were so accustomed to the widow's eccentricities that they were slow to be alarmed. It was only upon the Friday, when John Emms, the cobbler, found the same sinister silence prevailing in the house, that a fear of foul play came suddenly upon him. He ran round to Mr. Rose, her attorney, and Mr. Faith, who was a distant relation, and the three men returned to the house. On their way they picked up Police-constable Dillon, who accompanied them.

The front door was fastened and the windows snibbed, so the party made their way over the garden wall and so reached the back entrance, which they seem to have opened without difficulty. John Emms led the way, for he was intimately acquainted with the house. On the ground floor there was no sign of the old woman. The creak of their boots and the subdued whisper of their voices were the only sounds which broke the silence. They ascended the stair with a feeling of reassurance. Perhaps it was all right after all. It was quite probable that the eccentric widow might have gone on a visit. And then as they came upon the landing John Emms stood staring, and the others, peering past him, saw that which struck the hope from their hearts.

It was the footprint of a man dimly outlined in blood upon the wooden floor. The door of the front room was nearly closed, and this dreadful portent lay in front of it with the toes pointing away. The police-constable pushed at the door, but something which lay behind it prevented it from opening. At last by their united efforts they effected an entrance. There lay the unfortunate old woman, her lank limbs all asprawl upon the floor, with two rolls of wall-paper under her arm and several others scattered in front of her. It was evident that the frightful blows which had crushed in her head had fallen upon her unforeseen, and had struck her senseless in an instant. She had none of that anticipation which is the only horror of death.

*It was the footprint of a man
dimly outlined on the floor.*

The news of the murder of so well known an inhabitant caused the utmost excitement in the neighbourhood, and every effort was made to detect the assassin. A Government reward of £100 was soon raised to £300, but without avail. A careful examination of the house failed to reveal anything which might serve as a reliable clue. It was difficult to determine the hour of the murder, for there was reason to think that the dead woman occasionally neglected to make her bed, so that the fact that the bed was unmade did not prove that it had been slept in. She was fully dressed, as she would be in the evening, and it was unlikely that she would be doing business with wall-papers in the early morning. On the whole, then, the evidence seemed to point to the crime having been committed upon the Monday evening some time after seven. There had been no forcing of doors or windows, and therefore the murderer had been admitted by Mrs. Emsley. It was not consistent with her habits that she should admit anyone whom she did not know at such an hour, and the presence of the wall-papers showed that it was someone with whom she had business to transact. So far the police could hardly go wrong. The murderer appeared to have gained little by his crime, for the only money in the house, £48, was found concealed in the cellar, and nothing was missing save a few articles of no value. For weeks the public waited impatiently for an arrest, and for weeks the police remained silent though not inactive. Then an arrest was at last effected, and in a curiously dramatic fashion.

Amongst the numerous people who made small sums of money by helping the murdered woman there was one respectable-looking man, named George Mullins —rather over fifty years of age, with the straight back of a man who has at some period been well drilled. As a matter of fact, he had served in the Irish Constabulary, and had undergone many other curious experiences before he had settled down as a plasterer in the East-end of London. This man it was who called upon Sergeant Tanner, of the police, and laid before him a statement which promised to solve the whole mystery.

According to this account, Mullins had from the first been suspicious of Emms, the cobbler, and had taken steps to verify his suspicions, impelled partly by his love of justice and even more by his hope of the reward. The £300 bulked largely before his eyes. 'If this only goes right I'll take care of you,' said he, on his first interview with the police, and added, in allusion to his own former connection with the force, that he 'was clever at these matters.' So clever was he that his account of what he had seen and done gave the police an excellent clue upon which to act.

It appears that the cobbler dwelt in a small cottage at the edge of an old brick-field. On this brick-field, and about fifty yards from the cottage, there stood a crumbling outhouse which had been abandoned. Mullins, it seems, had for some time back been keeping a watchful eye upon Emms, and he had observed him carrying a paper parcel from his cottage and concealing it somewhere in the shed. 'Very likely,' said the astute Mullins, 'he is concealing some of the plunder which he has stolen.' To the police also the theory seemed not impossible, and so, on the following morning, three of them, with Mullins hanging at their heels, appeared at Emms's cottage, and searched both it and the shed. Their efforts, however, were in vain, and nothing was found.

They came upon a paper parcel of a very curious nature.

This result was by no means satisfactory to the observant Mullins, who rated them soundly for not having half-searched the shed, and persuaded them to try again. They did so under his supervision, and this time with the best results. Behind a slab in the outhouse they came on a paper parcel of a very curious nature. It was tied up with coarse tape, and when opened disclosed another parcel tied with waxed string. Within were found three small spoons and one large one, two lenses, and a cheque drawn in favour of Mrs. Emsley, and known to have been paid to her upon the day of the murder. There was no doubt that the other articles had also belonged to the dead woman. The discovery was of the first importance then, and the whole party set off for the police-station, Emms covered with confusion and dismay, while Mullins swelled with all the pride of the successful amateur detective. But his triumph did not last long.

At the police-station the inspector charged him with being himself concerned in the death of Mrs. Emsley.

'Is this the way that I am treated after giving you information?' he cried.

'If you are innocent no harm will befall you,' said the inspector, and he was duly committed for trial.

This dramatic turning of the tables caused the deepest public excitement, and the utmost abhorrence was everywhere expressed against the man who was charged not only with a very cold-blooded murder, but with a deliberate attempt to saddle another man with the guilt in the hope of receiving the reward. It was very soon seen that Emms at least was innocent, as he could prove the most convincing alibi. But if Emms was innocent who was guilty save the man who had placed the stolen articles in the outhouse? and who could this be save Mullins, who had informed the police that they were there? The case was prejudged by the public before ever the prisoner had appeared in the dock, and the evidence which the police had prepared against him was not such as to cause them to change their opinion. A damning series of facts were arraigned in proof of their theory of the case, and they were laid before the jury by Serjeant Parry at the Central Criminal Court upon the 25th of October, about ten weeks after the murder.

At first sight the case against Mullins appeared to be irresistible. An examination of his rooms immediately after his arrest enabled the police to discover some tape upon his mantelpiece which corresponded very closely with the tape with which the parcel had been secured. There were thirty-two strands in each. There was also found a piece of cobbler's wax, such as would be needed to wax the string of the inner parcel. Cobbler's wax was not a substance which Mullins needed in his business, so that time theory of the prosecution was that he had simply procured it in order to throw suspicion upon the unfortunate cobbler. A plasterer's hammer, which might have inflicted the injuries, was also discovered upon the premises, and so was a spoon which corresponded closely to the spoons which Mrs. Emsley had lost. It was shown also that Mrs. Mullins had recently sold a small gold pencil-case to a neighbouring barman, and two witnesses were found to swear that this pencil-case belonged to Mrs. Emsley and had been in her possession a short time before her death. There was also discovered a pair of boots, one of which appeared to fit the impression upon the floor, and medical evidence attested that there was some human hair upon the sole of it. The same medical evidence swore to a blood mark upon the gold pencil which had been sold by Mrs. Mullins. It was proved by the charwoman, who came upon Saturdays, that when she had been in the house two days before the murder Mullins had called, bringing with him some rolls of wall-paper, and that he had been directed by Mrs. Emsley to carry it up to the room in which the tragedy afterwards occurred. Now, it was clear that Mrs. Emsley had been discussing wall-papers at the time that she was struck down, and what more natural than that it should have been with the person who had originally brought them? Again, it had been shown that during the day Mrs. Emsley had handed to Mullins a certain key. This key was found lying in the same room as the dead body, and the prosecution asked how it could have come there if Mullins did not bring it.

So far the police had undoubtedly a very strong case, and they endeavoured to make it more convincing still by producing evidence to show that Mullins had been seen both going to the crime and coming away from it. One, Raymond, was ready to swear that at eight o'clock that evening he had caught a glimpse of him in the street near Mrs. Emsley's. He was wearing a black billy-cock hat. A sailor was produced who testified that he had seen him at Stepney Green a little after five next morning. According to the sailor's account his attention was attracted by the nervous manner and excited appearance of the man whom he had met, and also by the fact that his pockets were very bulging. He was wearing a brown hat. When he heard of the murder he had of his own accord given information to the police, and he would swear that Mullins was the man whom he had seen.

This was the case as presented against the accused, and it was fortified by many smaller points of suspicion. One of them was that when he was giving the police information about Emms he had remarked that Emms was about the only man to whom Mrs. Emsley would open her door.

'Wouldn't she open it for you, Mullins?' asked the policeman.

'No,' said he. 'She would have called to me from the window of the area.'

This answer of his-which was shown to be untrue-told very heavily against him at the trial.

It was a grave task which Mr. Best had to perform when he rose to answer this complicated and widely-reaching indictment. He first of all endeavoured to establish an alibi by calling Mullins's children, who were ready to testify that he came home particularly early upon that particular Monday. Their evidence, however, was not very conclusive, and was shaken by the laundress, who showed that they were confusing one day with another. As regards the boot, the counsel pointed out that human hair was used by plasterers in their work, and he commented upon the failure of the prosecution to prove that there was blood upon the very boot which was supposed to have produced the blood-print. He also showed as regards the bloodstain upon the pencil-case that the barman upon buying the pencil had carefully cleaned and polished it, so that if there was any blood upon it, it was certainly not that of Mrs. Emsley. He also commented upon the discrepancy of the evidence between Raymond, who saw the accused at eight in the evening in a black hat, and the sailor who met him at five in the morning in a brown one. If the theory of the prosecution was that the accused had spent the night in the house of the murdered woman, how came his hat to be changed? One or other or both the witnesses must be worthless. Besides, the sailor had met his mysterious stranger at Stepney Green, which was quite out of the line between the scene of the crime and Mullins's lodgings.

As to the bulging pockets, only a few small articles had been taken from the house, and they would certainly not cause the robbers pockets to bulge. There was no evidence either from Raymond or from the sailor that the prisoner was carrying the plasterer's hammer with which the deed was supposed to have been done.

And now he produced two new and very important witnesses, whose evidence furnished another of those sudden surprises with which the case had abounded. Mrs. Barnes, who lived in Grove Road, opposite to the scene of the murder, was prepared to swear that at twenty minutes to ten on Tuesday morning —twelve hours after the time of the commission of the crime, according to the police theory-she saw someone moving paper-hangings in the top room, and that she also saw the right-hand window open a little way. Now, in either of these points she might be the victim of a delusion, but it is difficult to think that she was mistaken in them both. If there was really someone in the room at that hour, whether it was Mrs. Emsley or her assassin, in either case it proved the theory of the prosecution to be entirely mistaken.

He had seen one Rowland, also a
builder, coming out of some house.

The second piece of evidence was from Stephenson, a builder, who testified that upon that Tuesday morning he had seen one Rowland, also a builder, come out of some house with wall-papers in his hand. This was a little after ten o'clock. He could not swear to the house, but he thought that it was Mrs. Emsley's. Rowland was hurrying past him when he stopped him and asked him —they were acquaintances-whether he was in the paper line.

'Yes; didn't you know that?' said Rowland.

'No,' said Stephenson, 'else I should have given you a job or two.'

'Oh, yes, I was bred up to it,' said Rowland, and went on his way.

In answer to this Rowland appeared in the box and stated that he considered Stephenson to be half-witted. He acknowledged the meeting and the conversation, but asserted that it was several days before. As a matter of fact, he was engaged in papering the house next to Mrs. Emsley's, and it was from that that he had emerged.

So stood the issues when the Chief Baron entered upon the difficult task of summing up. Some of the evidence upon which the police had principally relied was brushed aside by him very lightly. As to the tape, most tape consisted of thirty-two strands, and it appeared to him that the two pieces were not exactly of one sort. Cobbler's wax was not an uncommon substance, and a plasterer could not be blamed for possessing a plasterer's hammer. The boot, too, was not so exactly like the blood-print that any conclusions could be drawn from it. The weak point of the defense was that it was almost certain that Mullins hid the things in the shed. If he did not commit the crime, why did he not volunteer a statement as to how the things came into his possession? His remark that Mrs. Emsley would not open the door to him, when it was certain that she would do so, was very much against him. On the other hand, the conflicting evidence of the sailor and of the other man who had seen Mullins near the scene of the crime was not very convincing, nor did he consider the incident of the key to be at all conclusive, since the key might have been returned in the course of the day. On the whole, everything might be got round except the hiding of the parcel in the shed, and that was so exceedingly damning that, even without anything else, it amounted to a formidable case.

The jury deliberated for three hours and then brought in a verdict of 'Guilty,' in which the judge concurred. Some of his words, however, in passing sentence were such as to show that his mind was by no means convinced upon the point.

A verdict of "Guilty."

'If you can even now make it manifest that you are innocent of the charge,' said he, 'I do not doubt that every attention will be paid to any cogent proof laid before those with whom it rests to carry out the finding of the law.'

To allude to the possibility of a man's innocence and at the same time to condemn him to be hanged strikes the lay mind as being a rather barbarous and illogical proceeding. It is true that the cumulative force of the evidence against Mullins was very strong, and that investigation proved the man's antecedents to have been of the worst. But still, circumstantial evidence, even when it all points one way and there is nothing to be urged upon the other side, cannot be received with too great caution, for it is nearly always possible to twist it to some other meaning.

In this case, even allowing that the evidence for an alibi furnished by Mullins's children was worthless, and allowing also that Mr. Stephenson's evidence may be set aside, there remains the positive and absolutely disinterested testimony of Mrs. Barnes, which would seem to show that even if Mullins did the crime he did it in an entirely different way to that which the police imagined. Besides, is it not on the face of it most improbable that a man should commit a murder at eight o'clock or so in the evening, should remain all night in the house with the body of his victim, that he should do this in the dark-for a light moving about the house would have been certainly remarked by the neighbours-that he should not escape during the darkness, but that he should wait for the full sunlight of an August morning before he emerged?

After reading the evidence one is left with an irresistible impression that, though Mullins was very likely guilty, the police were never able to establish the details of the crime, and that there was a risk of a miscarriage of justice when the death sentence was carried out.

There was much discussion among the legal profession at the time as to the sufficiency of the evidence, but the general public was quite satisfied, for the crime was such a shocking one that universal prejudice was excited against the accused. Mullins was hanged on the 19th of November, and he left a statement behind him reaffirming his own innocence. He never attempted to explain the circumstances which cost him his life, but he declared in his last hours that he believed Emms to be innocent of the murder, which some have taken to be a confession that he had himself placed the incriminating articles in the shed. Forty years have served to throw no fresh light upon the matter.

The Case of Mr. George Edalji

The first sight which I ever had of Mr. George Edalji was enough in itself to convince me both of the extreme improbability of his being guilty of the crime for which he was condemned, and to suggest some at least of the reasons which had led to his being suspected.

He had come to my hotel by appointment, but I had been delayed, and he was passing the time by reading the paper. I recognized my man by his dark face, so I stood and observed him. He held the paper close to his eyes and rather sideways, proving not only a high degree of myopia, but marked astigmatism. The idea of such a man scouring fields at night and assaulting cattle while avoiding the police was ludicrous to any one who can imagine what the world looks like to eyes with myopia of eight dioptres-the exact value of Mr. Edalji's myopia, according to Mr. Kenneth Scott of Manchester. But such a condition, so hopelessly bad that no glasses availed in the open air gave the sufferer a vacant, bulge-eyed, staring appearance, which, when taken with his dark skin, must have made him seem a very queer man to the eyes of an English village, and therefore to be associated with any queer event. There, in a single physical defect, lay the moral certainty of his innocence, and the reason why he should become the scapegoat.

Before seeing him I had read the considerable literature which had been sent to me about his case. After seeing him I read still more, saw or wrote to every one who could in any way throw light upon the matter, and finally visited Wyrley and had a useful day's work upon the spot. The upshot of my whole research has been to introduce me to a chain of circumstances which seem so extraordinary that they are far beyond the invention of the writer of fiction. At all times in my inquiries I have kept before my mind the supreme necessity of following truth rather than any preconceived theory, and I was always prepared to examine any point against the accused with as much care as if it made for his innocence, but I have felt at last that it was an insult to my intelligence to hold out any longer against the certainty that there has been an inconceivable miscarriage of justice.

Let me tell the strange story from the beginning. I hope that the effect of my narrative will be to raise such a wave of feeling in this country as will make some public reconsideration of this case inevitable, for I am convinced that such reconsideration can only end in his complete acquittal and to his restoration to the rank of that honourable profession from which he has so unjustly been removed.

The story begins as far back as the year 1874, when the Rev. S. Edalji, a Church of England clergyman of Parsee origin, was married to Miss C. Stoneham. An uncle of the bride, as I understand it, held the gift of the living of Great Wyrley, which was a parish, half agricultural and half mining, about six miles from Walsall in Staffordshire. Through his uncle's influence Mr. Edalji became vicar of Great Wyrley, a cure which he has now held for thirty-one years, living a blameless life in the sight of all men. Placed in the exceedingly difficult position of a coloured clergyman in an English parish, he seems to have conducted himself with dignity and discretion. The only time that I can ever find that any local feeling was raised against him was during elections, for he was a strong Liberal in politics, and had been known to lend the church school-room for meetings. Some bitterness was aroused among the baser local politicians by this action.

There were three surviving children fro this union-George, who was born in 1876; Horace in 1879; and Maud in 1882. Of these Horace received a government post and was absent at the time when the long persecution to which the family had been subjected culminated in the tragedy which overwhelmed his brother.

In the year 1888, George Edalji being at that time 12 years of age, a number of threatening letters were received at the vicarage. The aid of the police was called, and an arrest was made. This was of the servant-maid at the vicarage, one Elizabeth Foster, who was accused, among other things, of writing up ribald sentences about her employers on outhouses and buildings. She was tried at Cannock in 1889, but her solicitor pleaded that it was all a foolish joke, and she was bound over to keep the peace. An attempt has been made to contend that she was not guilty, but I take it that no barrister could make such an admission without his client's consent. She and her friends were animated afterwards by bitter feelings of revenge, and there is good reason to believe that in this incident of 1888 is to be found the seed which led to the trouble of 1893-1895 and the subsequent trouble of 1903. The 1892-1895 letters openly championed Elizabeth Foster; the 1903 ones had no direct allusion to her, but a scurrilous postcard on August 4 contained the words: "Why not go on with your old game of writing things on walls?" this being the very offence Elizabeth Foster was charged with. The reader must remember that in 1888 George Edalji was a schoolboy of 12, and that the letters received at that date were in a formed handwriting, which could not possibly have been his.

In 1892 the second singular outbreak of anonymous letters began, some of which were published in the Staffordshire newspapers at the time by Mr. Edalji, in the hope that their style and contents might discover the writer. Many were directed to the vicarage, but many others were sent to different people in the vicinity, so malevolent and so ingenious that it seemed as if a very demon of mischief were endeavouring to set the parish by the ears. They were posted at Walsall, Cannock, and various other towns, but bore internal evidence of a common origin, and were all tainted with the Elizabeth Foster incident. They lasted for three years, and as they were accompanied by a long series of hoaxes it is really wonderful that they did not accomplish their proclaimed purpose, which was to drive their victim off his head.

On examination of such of these letters as I have been able to see, their prevailing characteristics are:

1. A malignant, diabolical hatred of the whole Edalji family, the 16-17-18-year-old George coming in for his fair share of the gross abuse. This hatred is insane in its intensity, and yet so coldly resolute that three years of constant persecution caused no mitigation. Here are extracts to illustrate the point: "I swear by God that I will murder George Edalji soon. The only thing that I care about in this world is revenge, revenge, revenge, sweet revenge, I long for, then I shall be happy in hell." "Every day, every hour, my hatred is growing against George Edalji." "Do you thing, you Pharisee, that because you are a parson God will absolve you from your iniquities?" "May the Lord strike me dead if I don't murder George Edalji." "Your damned wife." "Your horrid little girl." "I will descend into the infernal regions, showering curses upon you all." Such are a few of the phrases in which maniacal hatred of the Edalji family is shown.

2. The second characteristic of the letters is a frantic admiration, real or feigned, for the local police. There was a Sergeant Upton on duty in Cannock, who is eulogised in this way: "Ha, ha, hurrah for Upton! Good old Upton! Blessed Upton! Good old Upton! Upton is blessed! Dear old Upton!"

> "Stand up, stand up for Upton,
> Ye soldiers of the cross.
> Lift high your royal banner,
> It must not suffer loss."

"The following in this district we love truly-the police of Cannock in general." Again: "I love Upton. I love him better than life, because for my sake he lost promotion."

3. The third characteristic of these letters, besides hatred of Edalji and eulogy of the police, is real or simulated religious mania, taking the form, in some portions of the same letter, that the writer claims to be God, and in others that he is eternally lost in Hell. So consistent is this that it is hard to doubt that there was a real streak of madness in the writer.

4. The fourth remarkable characteristic of the letters is the intimacy of the writer with the names and affairs of the people in the district. As many as twenty names will sometimes be given, most of them with opprobrious epithets attached. No one can read them and doubt that the writer lived in the immediate neighbourhood, and was intimately acquainted with the people of whom he spoke.

One would imagine that under these circumstances there would be little difficulty in tracing the letters to their source, but, as a matter of fact, the handwriting was never recognised nor was the culprit discovered. The opinion was strongly held, however, by those who were most concerned, that there was a connexion with the former incident, and that the letters were done by some male ally or allies of the discharged maid.

While these letters had been circulating the life of the Edaljis had, as I have already said, been made miserable by a series of most ingenious and daring hoaxes, many of which might have seemed comic had it not been for the tragedy of such a persecution. In all sorts of papers the curious wants of the Rev. S. Edalji of Great Wyrley broke out by letter and by advertisement. Forgery caused no qualms to the hidden conspirator. Mr. Edalji became in these effusions an enterprising matrimonial agent, with a number of ladies, their charms and fortunes most realistically catalogued, whom he was ready to dispose of to any eligible bachelor. His house was advertised to be let for the most extraordinary purposes. His servant girl was summoned over to Wolverhampton to view the dead body of a non-existent sister supposed to be lying in a public house. Tradespeople brought cartloads of unordered good to the vicarage. A unfortunate parson from Norwich flew across to Great Wyrley on the urgent summons of the Rev. Shapurji Edalji, only to find himself the victim of a forgery. Finally, to the confusion of any one who imagines that the youth George Edalji was annoying himself and playing tricks upon his own people, there came a forged apology in the public press, beginning with the words: "We, the undersigned, G.E.T. Edalji and Frederick Brookes, both residing in the parish of Great Wyrley, do hereby declare that we were the sole authors and writers of certain offensive and anonymous letters received by various persons during the last twelve months." The apology then goes on to express regret for utterances against the favourite protégé of the unknown, Upton, the Sergeant of Police at Cannock, and also against Elizabeth Foster. This pretended apology was, of course, at once disowned by the Edaljis, and must, I think, convince any reasonable man, if there were already any room for doubt, that the Edaljis were not persecuting themselves in this maddening fashion.

Before leaving this subject of the anonymous letters of 1893, which breathe revenge against the Edalji family, I should like to quote and strongly emphasise two expressions which have a lurid meaning when taken with the actual outcome of the future.

On March 17, 1893, this real or pretended maniac says in a letter to the father:

"Before the and of this year your kid will be either in the graveyard or disgraced for life." Later, in the same letter, he says: "Do you think that when we want we cannot copy your kid's writing?"

Within ten years of the receipt of that letter the "kid," or George Edalji, had, indeed, been disgraced for life, and anonymous letters which imitated his handwriting had played a. part in his downfall. It is difficult after this to doubt that the schemer of 1893 was identical with the writer of the letters of 1903.

Among the many hoaxes and annoyances practiced during those years was the continual laying of objects within the vicarage grounds and on the window-sills or under the doors, done with such audacity that the culprit was more than once, nearly caught in the act. There was one of these incidents which I must allude to at some length, though it was trivial in itself, it has considerable importance as forming a link between the outrages of 1893 and of 1903, and also because it shows for the first time the very strong suspicion which Captain the Honorable G.A. Anson, Chief Constable of Staffordshire-influenced no doubt by those reports of his subordinates, which he may of may not have too readily believed-has shown toward George Edalji. Personally I have met with nothing but frankness and courtesy from Captain the Honorable G.A. Anson during the course of my investigation, and if in the search after truth I have to criticise any word or action of his, I can assure him that it is with regret and only in pursuit of what seems to me to be a clear duty.

On Dec. 12, 1902, at the very beginning of the series of hoaxes, a large key was discovered lying upon the vicarage door-step. This key was handed to the police, who, after diligent search, found it was a key which had been taken from Walsall Grammar School. The reason why I say that this incident has an important bearing upon the connection between the outrages of 1893 and those of 1903 is that the very first letter in the latter series proclaimed the writer to be a scholar at Walsall Grammar School. Granting that he could no longer be a scholar there if he were concerned in the hoaxes of 1893, it is still an argument that the same motive power lay behind each, since we find Walsall Grammar School obtruding itself in each case.

The incident of the key was brought before the chief constable of the county, who seems at once to have concluded that young George Edalji was the culprit. George Edalji was not a scholar at the Walsall School, having been brought up at Rugeley, and there does not appear to have been the slightest reason to suppose that he had procured a key from this six-miles-distant school and laid it on his own doorstep. However, here is a queer-looking boy, and here are queer doings, and here is a zealous constable, the very Upton whose praises were later to be so enthusiastically voiced by the writer of the letters. Some report was made, and the chief constable believed it. He took the course of writing in his own hand, over his own name, in an attempt to bluff the boy into a confession. Under date Jan. 23, 1898, he says to the father, in a letter which now lies before me: "Will you please ask your son George from whom the key was obtained which was found on your doorstep on Dec. 12? The key was stolen, but if it can be shown that the whole thing was due to some idle freak or practical joke I should not be inclined to allow any police proceedings to be taken in regard to it. If, however, the persons concerned in the removal of the key refuse to make any explanation of the subject, I must necessarily treat the matter in all seriousness as a theft. I may say at once that I shall not pretend to believe any protestations of ignorance which your son may make about the key. My information on the subject does not come from the police."

Considering the diabolical ingenuity of the hoaxer, it would seem probable that the information came directly or indirectly from him. In any case, it seems to have been false, or, at least, incapable of proof, as is shown by the fact that after these threats from the chief constable no action was taken. But the point to be noted is that as early as 1893, when Edalji was only 17, we have the police force of Staffordshire, through the mouth of their chief, making charges against him, and declaring in advance that they will not believe any protestation of innocence. Two years later, on July 25, 1895, the chief constable goes even further. Still writing to the father, he says: "I did not tell Mr. Perry that I know the name of the offender," (the writer of the letters and author of the hoaxes, "though I told him that I had my suspicions. I prefer to keep my suspicions to myself until I am able to prove them, and I trust to be able to obtain a dose of penal servitude for the offender; as, although great care has apparently been exercised to avoid, as far as possible, anything which would constitute any serious offense in law, the person who writes the letters has overreached himself in two or three instances, in such a manner as to render him liable to the most serious punishment. I have no doubt that the offender will be detected."

Now, it must be admitted that this is a rather sinister letter. It follows after eighteen months upon the previous one in which he accuses George Edalji by name. The letter was drawn from him by the father's complaint of gossip in the neighborhood, and the allusion to the skill of the offender in keeping within the law has a special meaning, in view of the fact that young Edalji was already a law student. Without mentioning a name, he assures Edalji's father that the culprit may get a dose of penal servitude. No doubt the chief constable honestly meant every word he said, and thought that he had excellent reasons for his conclusions; but the point is that if the Staffordshire police took this attitude toward young Edalji in 1895, what chance of impartiality had he in 1903, when a culprit was wanted for an entirely new set of crimes? It is evident that their minds were steeped in prejudice against him, and that they were in the mood to view his actions in the darkest light.

At the end of 1895 this persecution ceased. Letters and hoaxes were suddenly switched off. From that date till 1903 peace reigned in Wyrley. But George Edalji was resident at the vicarage all the time. Had he been the culprit there was no reason for change. But in 1903 the troubles broke out in a far more dangerous form than ever.

It was on Feb. 2, 1903, that the first serious outrage occurred at Wyrley. On that date a valuable horse belonging to Joseph Holmes was found to have been ripped up during the night. Two months later, on April 2, a cob belonging to Mr. Thomas was treated in a similar fashion, and a month after that a cow of Mrs. Bungay's was killed in the same way. Within a fortnight a horse of Badgers was terribly mutilated, and on the same day some sheep were killed. On June 6 two cows suffered the same fate, and three weeks later two valuable horses belonging to the Quinton Colliery Company were also destroyed. Next in order in this monstrous series of barbarities was the killing of a pony at Great Wyrley Colliery, for which George Edalji was arrested and convicted. His disappearance from the scene made no difference at all to the sequence of outrages, for on Sept. 21, between his arrest and his trial, another horse was dIsemboweled, and, as if expressly to confute the views of those who might say that this outrage was committed by confederates in order to affect the trial, the most diabolical deed of all was committed, after Edalji's conviction, on Nov. 3, when a horse and mare were found mutilated in the same field, an additional touch of horror being added by the discovery of a newly born foal some little distance from the mare.

Three, months later. on Feb. 8, 1904., another horse was found to be injured, and finally, on March 24. two sheep and a lamb were found mutilated, and a rough miner called Farrington was convicted upon entirely circumstantial evidence and condemned to three years. Now here the results of the police are absolutely illogical and incompatible. Their theory was that of a moonlighting gang. Edalji is condemned as one member of it, Farrington as another. But no possible connection can be proved or was ever suggested between Edalji and Farrington-the one a rude, illiterate miner, the other the son of the vicar and a rising professional man; the one a loafer at public houses, the other a total abstainer. It is certainly suggestive, presuming that Farrington did do the deed for which he was convicted, that he was employed at the Wyrley Colliery, and may have had to pass in going to his work that very pony which Edalji was supposed to have injured. It is also, it must be admitted, suggestive that while Edalji's imprisonment had no effect upon the outrages, Farrington was at once followed by their complete cessation. How monstrous, then, to contend, as the Home Office has done, that no new facts have arisen to justify a revision of Edalji's case. At the same time I do not mean to imply Farrington's guilt, of which I have grave doubts, but merely that, as compared with Edalji, a strong case could be made out against him.

New let me, before examining the outrage of Aug. 17, 1903, which proved so fatal to Edalji, give some account of the fresh epidemic of letters which broke out in the district. They were synchronous with the actual outrages, and there were details in them which made if possible, though by no means certain, that they were written by some one who was actually concerned in the crimes.

It cannot be said that there is absolute proof that the letters of 1903 were by the same hand as those of 1895, but there are points about their phrasing, about their audacity and violence of language, and finally, about the attentions which they bestow upon the Edalji family, which seem to point to a common origin. Only in this case the Rev. Edalji escapes, and it is the son-the same son who has been menaced in the first series with disgrace for life-who receives some of the communications and is referred to in the others. I may say that this series of letters presents various handwritings, all of which differ from the 1895 letters, put as the original persecutor was fond of boasting that he could change his handwriting, and even that he could imitate that of George Edalji, the variance need not be taken too seriously.

And now for the letters. They were signed by various names, but the more important purported to come from a young schoolboy named Greatorex. This youth denied all knowledge of them, and was actually away in the Isle of Man when some of them were written, as well as on Aug. 17, the date of the Wyrley outrage. It is a curious fact that this youth, in going up to Walsall every day to school, traveled with a certain number of school-fellows upon the same errand, and that the names of some of these school-fellows do find their way into these letters. In the same carriage traveled young Edalji upon some few occasions. "I have known accused by sight for three or four years," said Greatorex at the trial; "he has traveled in the same compartment with me and my schoolmates going to Walsall. This has not occurred many times during the last twelve months-about a dozen times, in fact." Now, at first sight one would think this was a point for the police, as on the presumption that Edalji wrote these anonymous letters it would account for the familiarity with these youths displayed in them. But since Edalji always went to business by the 7:30 train in the morning, and the boys took the same train every day, to find himself in their company twelve times in one year was really rather more seldom than one would expect. He drifted into their compartment as into any other, and he seems to have been in their company but not of it. Yet the anonymous letter writer knew that group of boys well, and the police by proving that George Edalji might have known them, seemed to make a distinct point against him.

The "Greatorex" letters to the police are all to the effect that the writer is a member of the gang for maiming cattle, that George Edalji is another member, and that he (Greatorex) is prepared to give away the gang if certain conditions are complied with. "I have got a dare-devil face and can run well, and when they formed that gang at Wyrley they got me to join. I knew all about horses and beasts and how to catch them best;...they said they would do me in if I funked it, so I did, and caught them both lying down at ten minutes to 3, and they roused up, and then I caught each under the belly, but they didn't spurt much blood, and one ran away, but the other fell.... Now I'll tell you who are in the gang, but you can't prove it without me. There is one named — —, from Wyrley, and a porter who they call — —, and he's had to stay away, and there's Edalji, the lawyer.... Now I have not told you who is at the back of them all, and I shan't unless you promise to do nothing at me. It is not true we always do it when the moon is young, and the one Edalji killed on April 11 was full moon." (It is worth mentioning here that there was no outrage at all within a week of that date.) "I've never been locked up yet, and I don't think any of the others have, except the Captain, so I guess they'll get off light."

I would draw attention in passing to the artistic touch of "ten minutes to three." This is realism overdone, as no mutilator on a dark night could readily consult his watch or care to remember the exact hour to a minute. But it corresponds closely to the remarkable power of imaginative detail —a rather rare gift-shown in the hoaxes of 1893-5.

In the next letter, also to the police, the unknown refers to his previous communication, but is a good deal more truculent and abusive than before. "There will be merry times at Wyrley in November," he says. "when they start on little girls, for they will do twenty wenches like the horse before next March. Don't think you are likely to catch them cutting the beasts; they go too quiet, and lie low for hours, till your men have gone....Mr. Edalji, him they said was locked up, is going to Brum on Sunday night to see the Captain, near Northfield, about how it's to be carried on with so many detectives about, and I believe they are going to do some cows in the daytime instead of at night....I think they are going to kill beasts nearer here soon, and I know Cross Keys Farm and West Cannock Farm are the two first on the list....You bloated blackguard, I will shoot you with father's gun through your thick head if you come in my way or go sneaking to any of my pals."

This letter was addressed. like the last, to:

The Sergeant,
Police Station,
Hednesford
Staffordshire,

bearing a Walsall postmark of July 10, 1903. Edalji is openly accused of the crimes in the letters, and yet the police put forward the theory that he himself wrote them, and founded upon the last sentence of them, which I have quoted, that second charge, which sounded so formidable in his indictment, viz., of threatening to murder Sergt. Robinson.

A few days previously a second police officer, Mr. Rowley of Bridgetown, had received another letter, evidently from the same hand. Here the detail as to the method of the crime is more realistic than ever, though no accusations against others are made. I quote this letter In extenso:

"Sir: A party whose initials you will guess will be bringing a new hook home by train from Walsall on Wednesday night, and he will have it in his special long pocket under his coat, and it you or your pals can get his coat pulled aside a bit you'll get sight of it, as it's an inch and a half longer than the one he threw out of sight when he heard some one a-slopin it after him this morning. He will come by that after five or six, or if he don't come home to-morrow he is sure on Thursday, an you have made a mistake not keeping all the plain clothesmen at hand. You sent them away too soon. Why, just think, he did it close where two of them were hiding only a few days gone by. But, Sir, he has got eagle eyes, and his ears is as sharp as a razor, and he is as fleet of foot as a fox, an as noiseless, an he crawls on all fours up to the poor beasts, an fondles them a bit, an then he pulls the hook smart across 'em, an out their entrails fly before they guess they are hurt. You want 100 detectives to run him in red-handed, because he is so fly, an knows every nook an corner. You know who it is, an I can prove it, but until £100 reward is offered for a conviction I shan't split no more."

There is, it must be admitted, striking realism in this account also, but a hook-unless it were a billhook or horticulture hook-could not under any circumstances have inflicted the injuries.

It seems absurd enough that these letters incriminating himself in such violent terms should be attributed to young Edalji, but the climax is reached when a most offensive postcard, handed in at Edalji's own business office, is also sworn to by the expert employed by the police as being in Edalji's own writing. This vile effusion, which cannot be reproduced in full, accuses Edalji of guilty relations with a certain lady, ending up with the words, "Rather go back to your old game of writing anonymous letters and killing cows and writing on walls."

Now this postcard was posted at Wolverhampton on Aug. 4, 1903. As luck would have it, Edalji and his sister had gone upon an excursion to Aberystwith that day, and were absent from very early morning till late at night. Here is the declaration of the station official upon the point:

On the night of 4th of August, 1903, and early morning of the 5th I was on duty at Rugeley Town Station, and spoke to Mr. George Edalji and his sister, who were in the train on their return from Aberystwith.

WILLIAM BULLOCK,
Porter-Signalman, Rugeley Town Station.

The station master at Wyrley has made a similar declaration.

It is certain, then, that this postcard could not have been by him, even had the insulting contents not made the supposition absurd. And yet it is included in that list of anonymous letters which the police maintained, and the expert declared, to be in Edalji's own handwriting. If this incident is not enough in itself to break down the whole case, so far as the authorship of the letters goes, then I ask, what in this world would be sufficient to demonstrate its absurdity?

Before leaving this postcard, let me say that it was advanced for the prosecution that if a card were posted at certain country boxes to be found within two and a half miles of Wyrley they would not be cleared till evening, and so would have the Wolverhampton mark of the next day. Thus the card might have been posted in one of these out-of-the-way boxes on the 3d and yet bear the mark of the 4th. This, however, will not do. The card has the Wolverhampton mark of the evening of the 4th, and was actually delivered in Birmingham on the morning of the 5th. Even granting that one day was Bank Holiday, you cannot stretch the dislocation of the postal service to the point that what was posted on the 3d took two days to go twenty miles.

Now during these six months, while Edalji was receiving these scurrilous letters, and while the police were receiving others accusing the young lawyer, you will naturally ask why did he not take some steps himself to prove his innocence and to find out the writer? He did, as a matter of fact, everything in his power. He offered a reward of £25 in the public press —a reward, according to the police theory, for his own apprehension. He showed the police the letters which he received, and he took a keen interest in the capture of the criminals, making the very sensible suggestion that bloodhounds should be used. It seems hardly conceivable that the prejudice of the police had risen to such a point that both these facts were alleged as suspicious circumstances against him, as though he were endeavoring to worm himself into their confidence, and so find out what measures they were taking for the capture of the offender. I am quite prepared to find that in these dialogues the quick-witted youth showed some impatience at their constant blunders, and that the result was to increase the very great malevolence with which they appear to have regarded him, ever since their chief declared, in 1895, "I shall not pretend to believe any protestations of ignorance which your son may make"

And now, having dealt with the letters of 1903, let me, before I proceed to the particular outrage for which Edalji was arrested and convicted, say a few words as to the personality of this unfortunate young man, who was, according to the police theory, an active member, if not the leading spirit, of a gang of village ruffians. Any one more absurdly constructed to play the role could not be imagined. In the first place he is a total abstainer, which in itself hardly seems to commend him to such a gang. He does not smoke. He is very shy and nervous. He is a most distinguished student, having won the highest legal prizes within his reach, and written at his early age a handbook of railway law. Finally, he is as blind as the proverbial bat, but the bat has the advantage of finding its way in the dark, which would be very difficult for him. To find a pony in a dark field, or, indeed, to find the field itself, unless it were easily approached, would be a hard task, while to avoid a lurking watcher would be absolutely impossible. I have myself practiced as an oculist, but I can never remember correcting so high a degree of astigmatic myopia as that which afflicts Mr. Edalji. "Like all myopics, Mr. Edalji," said an expert, "must find it at all times difficult to see clearly any objects more than a few inches off, and in dusk it would be practically impossible for him to find his way about any place with which he was not perfectly familiar." Fearing lest it might be thought that he was feigning blindness, I asked Mr. Kenneth Scott of Manchester Square to paralyze the accommodation by atropine, and then to take the result by means which were independent of the patient. Here is his report:

Right eye —8.75 Diop Spher.
—1.15 Diop cylind axis 90°.
Left eye —8.25 Diop Spher.

"I am prepared to testify as to the accuracy of the above under oath," says Mr. Kenneth Scott.

As to what such figures mean, I will bring it home to the uninitiated by saying that glass made up to that prescription would cause the normal healthy eye to see the world as Edalji's eyes always see it. I am prepared to have such a glass made up, and if any defender of the police will put it on at night, and will make his way over the'route the accused is alleged to have taken inside of an hour, I will admit that what seems to me absolutely impossible could be done. I may add that this blindness is a permanent structural condition, the same in 1903 as in 1900. I appeal to the practising oculists of this country, and I ask whether there is one of them who would not admit that such a condition of the eyes would make such a performance practically impossible, and that the circumstance must add enormously to a defense which is already overwhelmingly strong. And yet this all-important point was never made at the trial.

It is this studious youth, who touches neither alcohol nor tobacco, and is so blind that he gropes his way in the dusk, who is the dangerous barbarian who scours the country at night, ripping up horses. Is it not perfectly clear, looking at his strange, swarthy face and bulging eyes, that it is not the village ruffian, but rather the unfortunate village scapegoat, who stands before you?

I have brought the narrative down to the Aug. 17 outrage. At this period twenty constables and detectives had been brought into the district, and several, acting, I presume, upon orders from higher quarters, watched the vicarage at night

On Aug. 17 Edalji, following his own account, returned from his day's work at Birmingham-he had started in practice there as a lawyer-and reached his home about 6:30. He transacted some business, put on a blue serge coat, and then walked down to the bootmaker's in the village, where he arrived about 8:35, according to the independent evidence of John Hands, the tradesman in question. His supper would not be ready before 9:30, and until that hour he took a walk round, being seen by various people. His household depose to his return before supper time, and their testimony is confirmed by the statement of Walter Whitehouse, who saw the accused enter the vicarage at 9:25. After supper Edalji retired to bed in the same room as his father, the pair having shared an apartment for seventeen years. The old vicar was a light sleeper, his son was within a few feet of him, the whole house was locked up, and the outside watched by constables, who saw no one leave it. To show how close the inspection was, I may quote the words of Sergt. Robinson, who said: "I saw four men observing it when I was there....I could see the front door and side door. I should say no one could get out on the side I was watching without my seeing." This was before the night of the outrage, but it is inconceivable that if there was so close a watch then, there was none on the 17th.

By the police evidence there were no less than twenty men scattered about waiting for the offender. I may add at this point some surprise has been expressed that the vicar should sleep in the same room as his son with the door locked. They slept thus, and had done so for years, so that the daughter, whose health was precarious, might sleep with the mother, and the service of the house, there being only the one maid, should be minimized. Absurd emphasis has been placed by the police upon the door being locked at night. I can only suppose that the innuendo is that the vicar locked the door to keep his son from roving. Do we not all know that it is the commonest thing for nervous people to lock their doors whether alone or not, and Mr. Edalji has been in the habit of doing so all his long life. I have evidence that Mr. Edalji always locked his door before he slept with his son, and that he has continued to lock his door after his son left him. If, then-to revert to the evidence-it is possible for a person in this world to establish an alibi, it was successfully established by Edalji that night from 9:30 onward. Granting the perfectly absurd supposition that the old vicar connived at his son slipping out at night and ripping up cattle, you have still the outside police to deal with. On no possible supposition can George Edalji have gone out after 9:30.

And yet upon that night a pony had been destroyed at the Great Wyrley Colliery. Sergt. Parsons gave evidence that he saw the pony, apparently all right, at 11 o'clock at night. It was very dark, but he was not far off it. It was a wild night, with rain coming in squalls. The rain began about 12, and cleared about dawn, being very heavy at times. On the 18th, at 6:20. a lad named Henry Garrett, going to his work at the colliery, observed that the pony was injured. "It had a cut on the side," he said. "The blood was trickling from the wound. It was dropping pretty quickly."

The alarm was at once given. Constables appeared upon the scene. By 8:30 Mr. Lewis, a veterinary surgeon, was on the spot. "The wound," he deposed, "was quite fresh, and could not have been done further than six hours from the time he saw it." The least learned of laymen might be sure that if the pony was standing bleeding freely at 6 it could not have been so all night, as the drain must have exhausted it. And here, on the top of this obvious consideration, is the opinion of the surgeon that the injury was inflicted within six hours. Where George Edalji was during those six hours has already been shown beyond all possible dispute: so the whole bottom has dropped out of the case; but none the less the indefatigable police went on with their prearranged campaign.

That it was prearranged is evident, since it was not on account of evidence, but in search of evidence, that the constables raided the vicarage. The young lawyer had already started for his day's work in Birmingham. The startled parents were ordered to produce all the young man's clothing. The mother was asked for his dagger, but could produce nothing more formidable than a botany spud. A hunt was made for weapons, and a set of razors belonging to the vicar was seized. Some were said to be wet —a not uncommon condition for razors in the morning. Dark spots were perceived upon the back of one, but they proved upon chemical examination to be rust stains. Twelve men quartered the small garden, but nothing was found.

The clothes, however, were a more serious matter. One coat was seized by the police and declared to be damp. This is vigorously denied by the vicar, who handled the coat before it was removed. Damp is, of course, a relative term, and all garments may give some feeling of dampness after a rainy night, when the whole atmosphere is humid but if the condition had been caused by being out in the wild weather which prevailed that night it is certain that the coat would have been not damp but sopping wet. The coat, however, was not one which Edalji used outside, and the evidence of Mr. Hands was called to show that he had not worn it the night before. It was an old house coat, so stained and worn that it is not likely that an ambitious young professional man would, even in the lamp light, walk in the streets and show himself to his neighbors in such a garment. But it was these very stains which naturally attracted the attention of the police. There were some whitish stains-surely these must be the saliva of the unfortunate animal. They were duly tested and proved to be starch stains, probably from fish sauce or bread and milk. But there was something still more ominous upon this unhappy coat. There were, according to Inspector Campbell, "dark red or brown stains, right cuff much more stained than the left. There were other stains on each sleeve, further up, reddish brown or white. The coat was damp....There are other spots and stains upon it."

Now, the police try to make two points here: That the coat was damp and that there were stains which might have been the traces of the crime upon it. Each point is good in itself; but, unfortunately they are incompatible and mutually destructive. If the coat were damp, and if these marks were bloodstains contracted during the night then those stains were damp also, and the Inspector had only to touch them and then to raise his crimson ringer in the air to silence all criticism. But since he could not do so it is clear that the stains were not fresh; They fell twelve hours later into the capable hands of the police surgeon, and the sanguinary smears conjured up by the evidence of the constable diminished with absurd swiftness until they became "two stains in the centre of the right cuff, each about the size of a three-penny bit." This was declared by Dr. Butter to be mammalian blood. He found no more blood at all. How these small stains came there it is difficult to trace-as difficult as to trace a stain which I see now upon the sleeve of my own house jacket as I look down. A splash the gravy of underdone meat might well produce it. At any rate, it may most safely be said that the most adept operator who ever lived would not rip up horse with a razor upon a dark night and have only two three-penny-bit spots of blood to show for it. The idea is beyond argument.

But now, having exhausted the white stains and the dark stains, we come to the most damning portion of the whole indictment, though a careful consideration may change one's view as to who it is who is damned by it. The police claimed that they discovered horsehairs upon the coat. "On the sleeve, says Inspector Campbell, "I found brownish hairs, which look like horsehairs. There are some on now." Now, let us listen to the very clear statement of the vicar upon the subject. I transcribe in full:

"On Aug. 18, 1903, they called at the vicarage at about 8 o'clock in the morning, and in compliance with their request Mrs. Edalji showed them a number of garments belonging to her son, George Edalji. As soon as they saw the old coat they began to examine it, and Inspector Campbell put his finger upon one place and said that there was a hair there. Mrs. Edalji told him that it was not a hair, but a thread, and Miss Edalji. who was present then, remarked that it looked like a 'roving.' This was all that Inspector Campbell had said to them about the hair before I came down. When I saw him he told me that he had found horsehairs upon the coat. The coat was then spread out upon the desk in the study. I asked him to point out the place where the hairs were to be seen. He pointed out, a lower part of the coat, and said. 'There's a horsehair there.' I examined the place and said, 'There is no hair here at all.' Some further conversation followed, and then suddenly he put his finger upon another place on the coat nearer to where I was standing, and, drawing two straight lines with his finger, he said, 'Look here, Mr. Edalji, there's horsehair here.' I looked at the place for a moment, and in order to have more light upon it I took up the coat with both my hands and drew nearer to the window, and after carefully examining it I said to him, 'There is, to be sure, no hair here; it is a clear surface.' He then said that he wanted to take the coat with him, and I said, 'You can take the coat. I am satisfied there is no horsehair upon it.'

"Now I have said it over and over again, and I say it here once more, that there was absolutely no horsehair upon the coat. If there had been any I could not have failed to see it, and both Mrs. Edalji and Miss Edalji looked at the coat at the same time, and saw no hair of any sort upon it."

Incidentally it may be mentioned in connection with this statement, in which Miss Edalji entirely concurs, that we have the evidence of Miss Foxley, formerly of Newnham College, and then head mistress of the High School, that Miss Edalji was an exceedingly competent scientific observer. She adds, "Wilful misstatement on her part is as impossible in itself as it is inconsistent with her high principles and frank, straightforward character."

Now here is a clear conflict of evidence between two groups of interested people-the constables on the one hand, eager to build up their case; the household on the other, eager to confute this terrible accusation. Let us suppose the two statements balance each other. But is it not evident that there was only one course open for the police how to establish their point, and that if they did not avail themselves of it they put themselves out of court? Their obvious course was then and there to send for a referee-the police doctor, or any other doctor-and picking samples of the hair from the coat to have sealed them in an envelope, calling the newcomer to witness when and where they had been obtained. Such a proceeding must silence all doubt. But they did nothing of the kind. What they actually did do was to carry off the coat upon which three reputable witnesses have sworn there were no hairs. The coat then disappears from view for twelve hours. In the meantime the pony has been put out of its pain, and a portion or its hide was cut off with the hairs attached, and also secured by the police. The coat had been taken at eight in the morning. It was seen by Dr. Butter, the police surgeon at nine in the evening. At that hour Dr. Butter picked twenty-nine undoubted obvious horsehairs from its surface.

The prosecution have here to break their way through two strong lines of defense, each within the other. On the one hand, if Edalji had done the crime the evening before, it was his blue serge coat, and not his house coat, that he wore; as is shown by the independent evidence of Mr. Hands. In the second line of defense is the oath of the family that there were no hairs in the morning, which is strengthened by the failure of the police to demonstrate then and there a fact which could have been so easily and completely demonstrated. But now we are faced by the undoubted fact that the hairs were there, upon the cuffs and the left breast, by evening. Why was the coat not taken straight to the surgeon? Why was a piece of the animal's hide sent for before the coat was shown to Dr. Butter? One need not fly to extreme conclusions. It is to be remembered that the mere carrying of the hide and coat together may have caused the transference of hairs, or that the officers may themselves have gathered hairs on their clothes while examining the pony, and so unconsciously transferred them to the coat. But the fact that the hairs were found just on the cuffs and breast will still recur in the mind. It would be sad indeed to commit one injustice while trying to correct an other, but when the inevitable inquiry comes this incident must form a salient point of it.

There is one test which occurs to one's mind. Did the hairs correspond with the type, color, and texture of the hairs on the sample of hide? It they did, then they were beyond all question conveyed from the sample to the coat The cut was down on the belly, and the portion taken off was from the side of the cut. The under-hair of a horse differs greatly from longer, darker, harsher hair of the sides. A miscreant leaning against a horse would get the side hairs. If all the hairs on the coat were short belly hairs, then there is a suggestive fact for the inquiry. Dr. Butter must have compared their appearance.

Since writing the above I have been able to get the words of Dr. Butter's evidence They are quoted: "Numerous hairs on the jacket, which were similar in color, length, and structure to those on the piece of skin cut from the horse" In that case I say confidently-and all reflection must confirm it-that these hairs could not possibly be from the general body of the pony, but must have been transferred, no doubt unconsciously, from that particular piece of skin. With all desire to be charitable, the incident leaves a most unpleasant impression upon the mind.

If one could for one moment conceive one's self performing this barbarity, one would not expect to find hairs upon one's coat; There is no necessary connection at all. Anxious to avoid the gush of blood, one would imagine that one would hold off the animal with the flat of one bend and attack it with the other. To lean one's coat against its side would be to bring one's trousers and boots in danger of being soaked in blood.

So much for the saliva stains, the blood stains, and the hairs. There remain the questions of the trousers and the boots. The trousers were said by the police to be damp and stained with dark mud around the bottom. The boots were very wet. The boots were the same ones which Edalji had admittedly used during his sixty-minutes' walk upon the evening before. It was fine in the evening, but there had been heavy rain during the day, and puddles everywhere. Of course his boots were wet. The trousers were not a pair used the evening before, according to the family. No attempt was made to show blood marks on boots or trousers, though Mr. Sewell, a well-known veterinary surgeon deposed afterward that in making such an incision a skilled operator would wear an apron to prevent his clothes from being soaked. It is an interesting point, brought out by the evidence of some of the witnesses of the prosecution, that the mud at the place of outrage was yellow-red, a mixture of clay and sand, quite distinct from the road mud, which the police claim to have seen upon the trousers.

And now we come to the farce of the footprints. The outrage had occurred just outside a large colliery, and hundreds of miners going to their work had swarmed along every approach, in order to see the pony. The soft, wet soil was trampled up by them from 6 o'clock onward: yet on 4 o'clock of that afternoon, eight hours after the seizure of the boots, we have Campbell endeavoring to trace a similarity in tracks. The particular boot was worn at the heel, a fairly common condition, and some tracks among the multitude were down at the heel, and why should not the one be caused by the other? No cast was taken of the tracks. They were not photographed. They were not cut out for expert comparison. So little were they valued by Inspector Campbell that he did not even mention them to the Magistrates on the 19th. But in retrospect they grew more valuable, and they bulked large at the trial.

Now, once again, the police are trying to make e point which in itself would help them, but which is incompatible with their other points. Their original theory was that the crime was done before 9:30. There was heavy rain on and off all night. It is perfectly clear that any well-marked footsteps must have been left after the rain stopped, or when it had nearly stopped. Even granting that the earth was soft enough, as it was, to take footprints before then, this heavy rain would blur them to a point that would make identification by a worn-down heel absurd. What becomes, then, of all this elaborate business of the footmarks? Every point in this case simply crumbles to pieces as you touch it.

How formidable it all sounds-wet razor, blood on razor, blood and saliva and hair on coat, wet boots, footmark corresponding to boot-and yet how absolutely futile it all is when examined, There is not one single item which will bear serious criticism. Let us pass, however, from these material clues to those more subtle ones which the bearing or remarks of the youth may have furnished. These will bear examination even less than the others. As he waited upon the platform for the 7:30 train an ex-constable, now as innkeeper, named Markhew. came up to him and asked him to stay, as Inspector Campbell wished to see him. At the same moment some one announced that a fresh outrage had been committed, upon which Markhew says that Edalji turned away and smiled. Now, it is perfectly clear that a guilty man would have been much alarmed by the news that the police wished to see him, and that he would have done anything but smile on hearing of the outrage. Edalji's account is that Markhew said: "Can't you give yourself a holiday for one day?" on which Edalji smiled. Which is the more probable version I leave to the reader. The incident was referred to by the prosecuting counsel as "the prisoner's extraordinary conduct at the station."

He went to his office in Birmingham, and there, later in the day, he was arrested by the police.

On the way to the station, after his arrest, this unfortunate youth made another deadly remark: "I am not surprised at this. I have been expecting it for some time." It is not a very natural remark for a guilty man to make, if you come to think of it; but it is an extremely probable one from a man who believes that the police have a down him, and who is aware that he has been accused by name in malignant anonymous letters. What else would he have said? Next day and the following Monday he was before the Magistrates, where the police evidence, as already set forth was given.

The magisterial proceedings lasted till Sept. 4, off and on, when a prima facie case was made out, and the prisoner committed to the Staffordshire Quarter Sessions. How far a case of this importance should have been referred to any less tribunal than the Assizes I leave to legal opinion. Again the criminal made a remark which rose up in judgment against him. "I won't have bail," said he to Police Constable Meredith. "and when the next horse is killed it will not be by me."

In commenting upon this, Mr. Disturnal, the prosecuting counsel, said; "In refusing bail the prisoner made use of a very significant observation, and it went to suggest that the prisoner knew perfectly well what he was about when he refused bail." The inference here is that it was prearranged that a friend of Edalji's would do a fresh crime, in order to clear him. Was there ever a more unfair utterance! It was. "Heads I win, tails you lose!" If no crimes occur, then it is clear we have the villain under lock and key. If crimes do occur, then it is clear that he is deep in conspiracy with others. As a matter of fact, both Edalji's decision to remain in gaol and his remark were the most proper and natural things in the world. He believed that there was a strong conspiracy against him. In the face of the letters he had every reason to believe so. So long as he was in his cell he was safe, he thought, from this conspiracy. Perhaps another crime would be committed, and in that case, he thought, in the innocence of his heart, that it would clear him, In his wildest dreams he could never have imagined that such a crime would be fitted in as a link in the chain against him.

A crime was committed, and it occurred upon Sept. 21, between Edalji's committal and trial, whilst he lay in Stafford Gaol. The facts are these: Harry Green was the nineteen-year-old son of a farmer who lived somewhere between the vicarage and the scene of the outrage for which Edalji was convicted. He and Edalji knew each other slightly, as neighbors in the country must do, but how slight was their acquaintance may he shown by the fact that when, in the course, of my inquiry. I asked Edalji what Green's writing was like, he had to admit that he had never seen it. Consider the utter want of common ground between the two men, the purblind, studious, teetotal young lawyer of twenty-seven, and the young Yeomanry trooper of nineteen, one of a set of boisterous young fellows, who made a centre of mirth and also of mischief at each annual training. Edalji entered no public house, and was at work from early morning to late at night. Where was there room for that blood-brotherhood which would make the one man risk any danger and sacrifice his own horse for the sake of the other?

Green's charger was found disemboweled. It was not a very valuable animal. In one estimate it is placed at five pounds. Whether it was insured or not there is a conflict of evidence. For days there were scare and conjecture. Then, at the end of that time, it was known that Green had signed a confession which admitted that he had himself killed his own horse. That confession undoubtedly exists, but Green, having had a week or two to think things over, and having in the meantime got a ticket to South Africa, suddenly went back on his own confession, and declared, with much circumstantiality of detail, that he had not done it, and that the confession had been bullied out of him by the police. One or other statement of Green's must be a falsehood, and I have sufficient reason myself, in the shape of evidence which has been set before me, to form a very clear opinion what the actual facts of the case were. When a final clearing of the case arrives, and there is a renewed inquiry on the basis that Edalji is innocent, and that the actual perpetrators have never been punished, there are many facts which may be laid before the authority who conducts it. Meanwhile the task which lies immediately before me is not to show who committed the crimes–though that, I think, is by no means an insuperable problem–but that Edalji did not and could not have committed them. I will leave young Green there, with his two contradictory statements, and I will confine myself to his relation with the case, whichever of the statements is true.

And, first of all, here are the police who claim to hold his written confession. Then why did they not prosecute? It will not do to say, that it is not a crime to kill your own horse. It is not a crime to shoot your own horse from humane motives, but it is at all times a crime, as the Society for the Prevention of Cruelty to Animals would very quickly show, to disembowel a horse on a dark night, be it fifty times your own. Here is an outrage of the same sort which has convulsed the countryside for so many months. It is brought home by his own confession to the offender, and yet the police refuse to prosecute and connive at the man's flight from the country. But why? If it was not that the prosecution of Green would bring out facts which would interfere with the successful prosecution of Edalji, then, again, I ask, why?

Far be it from me to be unjust to the police, but again it is their own really extraordinary behavior which drives one to seek for hypotheses. The Home Office says that all inquiry has been made in this case, and that everything has been investigated and the matter closed. That is the official answer I received only a fortnight ago. Then can the Home Office give any good reason why Green was not prosecuted? The point is a very vital one.

Green was present at Edalji's trial, was not called, and left afterward for South Africa. He had been subpoenaed by the police, and that, no doubt, was what prevented the defense from calling him. But had they done so, and had he spoken in public as he has spoken in private, there would have been an end of all possibility, according to my information, of the great miscarriage which ensued.

It may be noted before leaving this extraordinary incident that the reason given by Green in his confession was that the horse had to be killed, having been injured in the Yeomanry training, but nowhere has he ever said a word to suggest that he was acting in collusion with George Edalji.

And now at last we come to the trial. Here, as at every point of this extraordinary case, there are irregularities which will be more fitly dealt with by a lawyer. Suffice it that though the case was of such importance that it is generally thought that it should not have been at Quarter Sessions at all, it was at the lesser of the courts which make up that tribunal that it was at last tried. In Court A a skilled lawyer presided. Sir Reginald Hardy, who conducted Court B, had no legal training. I have not a word to say against his desire to be impartial and fair, but here was a young man, accused of one of a series of crimes for which the whole country was longing to find some one who might be made an example of. The jury would naturally have the same feelings as their fellow-citizens. Hence it was peculiarly necessary to have a cold legal mind to cool their ardor and keep them on firm ground of fact, far from prejudice and emotion. Yet it was in the court of the layman that the case was tried.

The ground over which the prosecution advanced is already familiar to the reader. We have the clothes which have now become "wet." They were merely "damp" in the previous inquiry, and we have the word of the vicar that this dampness was imperceptible to him, coupled with the fact that any bloodstains would then have been liquid. We have the down-at-heel boot, which was fitted into impressions which must have been made after rain, whereas the whole police theory was that the crime was committed before the rain. We have the bloodstains which sank from smears in to two threepenny-bit patches, and we have the hairs which made their appearance thirteen hours after the coat had been in the hands of the police, and after it had been associated with the strip of horse's hide. Then came the letters. There was a strong probability that whoever wrote the letters knew something of the crimes. What matter that the letters actually accused Edalji himself and vilified him in all sorts of ways? What matter that one villainous postcard in the same writing as the others was posted at Wolverhampton when he was at Aberystwith? What matter that in the original series of anonymous letters the writer had said: "Do you think we cannot imitate your kid's writing?"

None of these things weighed as compared with the expression of opinion by an expert that the letters were in George Edalji's own witting. As the unfortunate prisoner listened to such an opinion he must have felt that he was in some nightmare dream. And who was the expert who expressed these views which weighed so heavily with the jury? It was Mr. Thomas Gurrin. And what is the record of Mr. Thomas Gurrin? His nemesis was soon to come. Within a year he had to present himself before the Beck Committee, and admit the terrible fact that through his evidence an innocent man had suffered prolonged incarceration. Does this fact alone not convince my readers that an entire reconsideration of the Edalji case is a most pressing public duty?

There is absolutely the whole evidence-the coat-boot-razor business, the letter business. the so-called incriminating expression which I have already analyzed, and the one fact, which I admit did really deserve consideration, that a group or schoolboys with whom once a month young Edalji may have traveled were known also to the writer of the letters. That is all. I have shown what each link is worth. And on that evidence a young gentleman, distinguished already in an honorable profession, was torn from his family, suffered all the indignities of a convict, was immured for three of the best years of his life, was struck from the roll on which with such industry and self-denial he had written his name, and had every torture made ten-fold more bitter by the thought of the vicar at home, of his mother and of his sister, so peculiarly sensitive, from their position in the church, to the scoff and the derision of those around them. It is a tale which makes a man hot with indignation as he reads it.

One word as to the evidence of the family, upon which so much depends. It has been asserted that it was given in a peculiar way, which shook the confidence of the jury. I have had some experience of the Edaljis, and I can say with confidence that what seemed peculiar to the jury arose from extreme anxiety to speak the absolute, exact truth. An experienced barrister who knew them well remarked to me that they were the most precisely truthful people he had ever met —"bad witnesses," he added, "as they are so conscientious that they lay undue stress upon any point of doubt."

It must be admitted that the defense was not as strong as it might have been made, which does not seem to have been due to any shortcomings of the counsel so much as to a deficiency in the supply of information. The fact is that the consciousness of innocence was in this case a danger, as it caused some slackness in guarding every point. So far as I can find, the whole story of the early persecutions of 1888 and of 1893-5 was not gone into, nor was their probable connection with that of 1903 pointed out. The blindness of Edalji, a most vital fact, was not supported by an array of evidence; indeed, I think that it was hardly mentioned at all. At all points one finds things which might have been better, but even granting that, one cannot but feel the amazement, which Sir George Lewis has voiced, when the jury brought in "Guilty," and Sir Reginald Hardy sentenced the prisoner to seven years.

Now, once again, let me state the double dilemma of the police, before I leave this portion of my statement. Either Edalji did the crime before 10 o'clock that night or after 10 o'clock that night. The latter case must be laughed out of a common-sense court by the fact that his father, the vicar, spent the night within a few feet of him, that the small vicarage was bolted and barred, no one being heard to leave it, and that the police watchers outside saw no one leave it. If that does not establish an alibi, what could? On the other hand, supposing that he did it before 10 or rather before 9:30, the time of his return home. You have to face the supposition that after returning from a long day's work in Birmingham. he sallied out in a coat which he was only known to wear in the house, performed a commonplace mission at the bootshop in the village, then, blind as he was, hurried off for three-quarters of a mile through difficult, tortuous ways, with fences to climb and railway lines to cross (I can answer for it, having myself trod every foot of it) to commit a ghastly and meaningless crime, entirely foreign to his studious and abstinent nature; that he then hurried back another three-quarters of a mile to the vicarage, arrived so composed and tidy as to attract no attention, and sat down quietly to the family supper, the whole expedition from the first to the last being under an hour.

The mere statement of this alternative supposition seems grotesque enough, but on the top of the inherent improbability you are up against the hard facts that the pony was bleeding freely in the morning, and could not have so bled all night, that the veterinary surgeon deposed that the wound could not possibly be more than six hours old, no other veterinary surgeon being called to contradict this statement, and that the footprints on which the police relied were worthless unless left after the rain, which began at twelve. Add to this that the pony was seen standing apparently all right by the police themselves at 11 o'clock, and the case then seems to me to be overpoweringly convincing. Take whichever supposition you like, and I say that it is demonstrably false, and an insult to common sense to suppose that George Edalji committed the crime for which, through the action of the Staffordshire police, the error of an expert, and the gross stupidity of a jury, he has been made to suffer so cruelly.

I do not know that there is much to add, save bare recital of the events which have occurred since then. After Edalji's conviction the outrages continued unabated, and the epidemic of anonymous letters raged as ever. The November outrage upon Mr. Stanley's horses was never traced, but there was some good local information as to the author or that crime, and a widespread conviction in the district, which may have been utterly unjust, that the police were not too anxious to push the matter, as any conviction would certainly disturb the one which they had already obtained. This incident, also, will furnish some evidence for the coming inquiry. Finally, in March, 1904, a man, named Farrington, was convicted for injuring some sheep. No attempt has ever been made to trace any connection between this man and Edalji.

In the Green case not only was there no attempt to prove complicity between Green and Edalji, but I have evidence to show that the police had a most positive statement from Green that he had nothing to do with Edalji, obtained under circumstances which make it perfectly convincing. And yet, in face of this fact, Mr. Disturnal, the mouthpiece of the police at the trial, was permitted to say, referring to this outrage: "The letters which would be read would show that the writer of them was not acting alone, but in conjunction with some other people, and he put it to the jury, what was more likely than that, if there was a gang operating in the way suggested, one of its members would commit a similar outrage in order to create evidence for the defense?" Counsel, no doubt, spoke according to his instructions; but what are we to think of those from whom such instructions issued, since they had the clearest proof that there was no connection between Green and Edalji! Such incidents shake one's confidence in British Justice to the very foundations, for it is clear that the jury, already prejudiced by the nature of the crimes, were hoodwinked into giving their conviction.

A few words as to the sequel. The friends of the prisoner, organized and headed by Mr. R.D. Yelverton (late Chief Justice of the Bahamas), to whose long, ceaseless, and unselfish exertions Edalji will owe so much when the hour of triumph comes, drew up a memorial to the Home Secretary, setting forth some of the facts as here recorded. This petition for reconsideration was signed by 10,000 people, including hundreds of lawyers and many K.C.'s, and was reinforced by the strongest letters testifying to Edalji's character from men who must have known him intimately, including Mr. Denning, his schoolmaster; Mr. Ludlow, the solicitor with whom he was for five years articled; the Honorary Secretary and Reader of the Birmingham Law Society, and many others. Now, every man of the world will admit that the school-master's testimony is of very great importance, for any traits of cruelty will show themselves most clearly at that age. This is what Mr. Denning says: "During the five years your son George was here I have never known him to commit any acts of cruelty or unkindness. I have always found him a thoroughly upright and well-principled youth, in whom I could place every confidence." Grier, his schoolmate, writes: "He was several years older than myself, but always treated me with great kindness. I never knew him cruel to any animal, and from what I knew of him then-for I came to know him well —I should say he was quite incapable of any act of cruelty." How foolish the loose gossip and surmise of Stafford seem in the face of page after page of testimonials such as these!

The memorial had no effect, and some inquiry should certainly be made as to how its fate was determined. It would be indeed a vicious circle if a police prosecution, when doubted, is referred back again to the police for report. I cannot imagine anything more absurd and unjust; in an Oriental despotism than this. And yet any superficial independent investigation, or even a careful perusal of the memorial must have convinced any reasonable human being. The friends of Edalji, headed by Mr. Yelverton, naturally demanded to see the dossier at the Home Office, but, as in the Beck case, the seekers after justice were denied access to the very documents which they needed in order to prove their case and confute their opponents.

I have said it was as in the Beck case. I might well have gone to a more classic example. for in all its details this seems to me to form a kind of squalid Dreyfus case. The parallel is extraordinarily close. You have a Parsee, instead of a Jew, with a promising career blighted, in each case the degradation from a profession and the campaign for redress and restoration, in each case questions of forgery and handwriting arise, with Esterhasy in the one, and the anonymous writer in the other. Finally, I regret to say, that in the one case you have a have a clique of French officials going from excess to excess in order to cover an initial mistake, and that in the other you have the Staffordshire police acting in the way I have described.

And that brings me to what is the most painful part of my statement, and one which I would be most glad to shirk were it possible for me to do so. No account of the case is complete which does not deal with the attitude taken up by Captain Anson, Chief Constable of Staffordshire, against this unhappy man. It must, I suppose, have taken its root in those far-off days from 1892 to 1895, when Edalji was little more than a boy, and when Sergeant Upton, for reasons which make a tale by themselves, sent reports against him to his superior at ' Stafford. It was at that early date that Captain Anson delivered those two memorable dicta: "You may tell your son at once that I will not believe any profession of ignorance," and "I will endeavor to get the offender a dose of penal servitude."

Now, I have no doubt Captain Anson was quite honest in his dislike and unconscious of his own prejudice. It would be folly to think otherwise. But men in his position have no right to yield to such feelings. They are too powerful, others are too weak, and the oonsequences are too terrible. As I trace the course of events this dislike of their chief's filtered down until it came to imbue the whole force, and when they had George Edalji they did not give him the most elementary justice, as is shown by the tact that they did not prosecute Green at a time when his prosecution would have endangered the case against Edalji.

I do not know what subsequent reports prevented justice from being done at the Home Office-there lies the wickedness of the concealed dossier) —but this I do know, that, instead of leaving the fallen man alone, every possible effort was made after the conviction to blacken his character, and that of his father, so as to frighten off any one who might be inclined to investigate his case. When Mr. Yelverton first took it up, he had a letter over Capt. Anson's own signature, saying, · under date Nov. 8, 1903: "It is right to tell you that you will find it a simple waste of time to attempt to prove that Edalji could not, owing to his position and alleged good character, have been guilty of writing offensive and abominable letters. His father is as well aware as I am of his proclivities in the direction of anonymous writing, and several other people have personal knowledge on the same subject?"

Now, both Edalji and his father declare on oath that the former never wrote an anonymous letter in his life, and on being applied to by Mr. Yelverton for the names of the "several other people" no answer was received. Consider that this letter was written immediately after the conviction, and that it was intended to nip in the bud the movement in the direction of mercy. It is certainly a little like kicking a man when he is down.

Since I took up the case I have myself had a considerable correspondence with Capt. Anson. I find myself placed in a difficult position as regards these letters, for while the first was marked "Confidential," the others have no reserve. One naturally supposes that when a public official writes upon a public matter to a perfect stranger the contents are for the public. No doubt one might also add, that when an English gentleman makes most damaging assertions about other people he is prepared to confront these people, and to make good his words. Yet the letters are so courteous to me personally that it makes it exceedingly difficult for me to use them for the purpose of illustrating my thesis-viz., the strong opinion which Capt. Anson had formed against the Edalji family. One curious example of this is that during fifteen years that the vicarage has been a centre of debate, the chief constable has never once visited the spot or taken counsel personally with the inmates.

For three years George Edalji endured the privations of Lewes and of Portland. At the end of that time the indefatigable Mr. Yelverton woke the case up again, and *Truth* had an excellent series of articles demonstrating the impossibility of the man's guilt. Then the case took a new turn, as irregular and illogical as those which had preceded it. At the end of his third year, out of seven, the young man, though in good health, was suddenly released without pardon. Evidently the authorities were shaken, and compromised with their conscience in this fashion. But this cannot be final. The man is guilty, or he is not. If he is he deserves every day of his seven years. If he is not, then we must have apology, pardon, and restitution. There can obviously be no middle ground between these extremes.

And what else is needed besides this tardy justice to George Edalji? I should say that several points suggest themselves for the consideration of any small committee. One is the reorganization of the Staffordshire Constabulary from end to end; a second is an inquiry into any irregularity of procedure at Quarter Sessions; the third and most important is a stringent inquiry as to who is the responsible man at the Home Office, and what is the punishment for his delinquency, when in this case, as in that of Beck, justice has to wait for years upon the threshold and none will raise the latch. Until each and all of these questions is settled a dark stain will remain upon the administrative annals of this country.

I have every sympathy with those who deprecate public agitations of this kind on the ground that they weaken the power of the forces which make for law and order, by shaking the confidence of the public. No doubt they do so. But every effort has been made in this case to avoid this deplorable necessity. Repeated applications for justice under both administrations have met with the usual official commonplaces, or have been referred back to those who are obviously interested parties.

Amid the complexity of life and the limitations of intelligence any man may do an injustice, but how is it possible to go on again and again reiterating the same one? If the continuation of the outrages, the continuation of the anonymous letters, the discredit cast upon Gurrin as an expert, the confession of a culprit that he had done a similar outrage, and, finally the exposition of Edalji's blindness, do not present new facts to modify a jury's conclusion, what possible new fact would do so? But the door is shut in our faces. Now we turn to the last tribunal of all, a tribunal which never errs when the facts are fairly laid before them, and we ask the public of Great Britain whether this thing in to go on.

ARTHUR CONAN DOYLE, Undershaw, Hindhead, January, 1907.

The Case of Oscar Slater

It is impossible to read and weigh the facts in connection with the conviction of Oscar Slater in May, 1909, at the High Court in Edinburgh, without feeling deeply dissatisfied with the proceedings, and morally certain that justice was not done. Under the circumstances of Scotch law I am not clear how far any remedy exists, but it will, in my opinion, be a serious scandal if the man be allowed upon such evidence to spend his life in a convict prison. The verdict which led to his condemnation to death, was given by a jury of fifteen, who voted; Nine for "Guilty," five for "Non-proven," and one for "Not Guilty." Under English law, this division of opinion would naturally have given cause for a new trial. In Scotland the man was condemned to death, he was only reprieved two days before his execution, and he is now working out a life sentence in Peterhead convict establishment. How far the verdict was a just one, the reader may judge for himself when he has perused a connected story of the case. There lived in Glasgow in the year 1908, an old maiden lady named Miss Marion Gilchrist. She had lived for thirty years in the one flat, which was on the first floor in 15, Queen's Terrace. The flat above hers was vacant, and the only immediate neighbours were a family named Adams, living on the ground floor below, their house having a separate door which was close alongside the flat entrance. The old lady had one servant, named Helen Lambie, who was a girl twenty-one years of age. This girl had been with Miss Gilchrist for three or four years. By all accounts Miss Gilchrist was a most estimable person, leading a quiet and uneventful life. She was comfortably off, and she had one singular characteristic for a lady of her age and surroundings, in that she had made a collection of jewelry of considerable value. These jewels, which took the form of brooches, rings, pendants, etc., were bought at different times, extending over a considerable number of years, from a reputable jeweller. I lay stress upon the fact, as some wild rumour was circulated at the time that the old lady might herself be a criminal receiver. Such an idea could not be entertained. She seldom wore her jewelry save in single pieces, and as her life was a retired one, it is difficult to see how anyone outside a very small circle could have known of her hoard. The value of this treasure was about three thousand pounds. It was a fearful joy which she snatched from its possession, for she more than once expressed apprehension that she might be attacked and robbed. Her fears had the practical result that she attached two patent locks to her front door, and that she arranged with the Adams family underneath that in case of alarm she would signal to them by knocking upon the floor.

It was the household practice that Lambie, the maid, should go out and get an evening paper for her mistress about seven o'clock each day. After bringing the paper she then usually went out again upon the necessary shopping. This routine was followed upon the night of December 21st. She left her mistress seated by the fire in the dining-room reading a magazine. Lambie took the keys with her, shut the flat door, closed the hall door downstairs, and was gone about ten minutes upon her errand. It is the events of those ten minutes which form the tragedy and the mystery which were so soon to engage the attention of the public.

According to the girl's evidence, it was a minute or two before seven when she went out. At about seven, Mr. Arthur Adams and his two sisters were in their dining-room immediately below the room in which the old lady had been left. Suddenly they heard "a noise from above, then a very heavy fall, and then three sharp knocks." They were alarmed at the sound, and the young man at once set off to see if all was right. He ran out of his hall door, through the hall door of the flats, which was open, and so up to the first floor, where he found Miss Gilchrist's door shut. He rang three times without an answer. From within, however, he heard a sound which he compared to the breaking of sticks. He imagined therefore that the servant girl was within, and that she was engaged in her household duties. After waiting for a minute or two, he seems to have convinced himself that all was right. He therefore descended again and returned to his sisters, who persuaded him to go up once more to the flat. This he did and rang for the fourth time. As he was standing with his hand upon the bell, straining his ears and hearing nothing, someone approached up the stairs from below. It was the young servant-maid,

Helen Lambie, returning from her errand. The two held council for a moment. Young Adams described the noise which had been heard. Lambie said that the pulleys of the clothes-lines in the kitchen must have given way. It was a singular explanation, since the kitchen was not above the dining-room of the Adams, and one would not expect any great noise from the fall of a cord which suspended sheets or towels. However, it was a moment of agitation, and the girl may have said the first explanation which came into her head. She then put her keys into the two safety locks and opened the door. At this point there is a curious little discrepancy of evidence. Lambie is prepared to swear that she remained upon the mat beside young Adams. Adams is equally positive that she walked several paces down the hall. This inside hall was lit by a gas, which turned half up, and shining through a coloured shade, gave a sufficient, but not a brilliant light. Says Adams: "I stood at the door on the threshold, half in and half out, and just when the girl had got past the clock to go into the kitchen, a well-dressed man appeared. I did not suspect him, and she said nothing; and he came up to me quite pleasantly. I did not suspect anything wrong for the minute. I thought the man was going to speak to me, till he got past me, and then I suspected something wrong, and by that time the girl ran into the kitchen and put the gas up and said it was all right, meaning her pulleys. I said: 'Where is your mistress?' and she went into the dining-room. She said: 'Oh! come here!' I just went in and saw this horrible spectacle."

The spectacle in question was the poor old lady lying upon the floor close by the chair in which the servant had last seen her. Her feet were towards the door, her head towards the fire-place. She lay upon a hearth-rug, but a skin rug had been thrown across her head. Her injuries were frightful, nearly every bone of her face and skull being smashed. In spite of her dreadful wounds she lingered for a few minutes, but died without showing any sign of consciousness.

The murderer when he had first appeared had emerged from one of the two bedrooms at the back of the hall, the larger, or spare bedroom, not the old lady's room. On passing Adams upon the doormat, which he had done with the utmost coolness, he had at once rushed down the stair. It was a dark and drizzly evening, and it seems that he made his way along one or two quiet streets until he was lost in the more crowded thoroughfares. He had left no weapon nor possession of any sort in the old lady's flat, save a box of matches with which he had lit the gas in the bedroom from which he had come. In this bedroom a number of articles of value, including a watch, lay upon the dressing-table, but none of them had been touched. A box containing papers had been forced open, and these papers were found scattered upon the floor. If he were really in search of the jewels, he was badly informed, for these were kept among the dresses in the old lady's wardrobe. Later, a single crescent diamond brooch, an article worth perhaps forty or fifty pounds, was found to be missing. Nothing else was taken from the flat. It is remarkable that though the furniture round where the body lay was spattered with blood, and one would have imagined that the murderer's hands must have been stained, no mark was seen upon the half-consumed match with which he had lit the gas, nor upon the match box, the box containing papers, nor any other thing which he may have touched in the bedroom.

We come now to the all-important question of the description of the man seen at such close quarters by Adams and Lambie. Adams was short-sighted and had not his spectacle3 with him. His evidence at the trial ran thus: "He was a man a little taller and a little broader than I am, not a well-built man but well featured and clean-shaven, and I cannot exactly swear to his moustache, but if he had any it was very little. He was rather a commercial traveller type, or perhaps a clerk, and I did not know but what he might be one of her friends. He had on dark trousers and a light overcoat. I could not say if it were fawn or grey. I do not recollect what sort of hat he had. He seemed gentlemanly and well-dressed. He had nothing in his hand so far as I could tell. I did not notice anything about his way of walking."

Helen Lambie, the other spectator, could give no information about the face (which rather bears out Adams' view as to her position), and could only say that he wore a round cloth hat, a three-quarter length overcoat of a grey colour, and that he had some peculiarity in his walk. As the distance traversed by the murderer within sight of Lambie could be crossed in four steps, and as these steps were taken under circumstances of peculiar agitation, it is difficult to think that any importance could be attached to this last item in the description.

It is impossible to avoid some comment upon the actions of Helen Lambie during the incidents just narrated, which can only be explained by supposing that from the time she saw Adams waiting outside her door, her whole reasoning faculty had deserted her. First, she explained the great noise heard below: "The ceiling was like to crack," said Adams, by the fall of a clothes-line and its pulleys of attachment, which could not possibly, one would imagine, have produced any such effect. She then declares that she remained upon the mat, while Adams is convinced that she went right down the hall. On the appearance of the stranger she did not gasp out: "Who are you?" or any other sign of amazement, but allowed Adams to suppose by her silence that the man might be someone who had a right to be there. Finally, instead of rushing at once to see if her mistress was safe, she went into the kitchen, still apparently under the obsession of the pulleys. She informed Adams that they were all right, as if it mattered to any human being; thence she went into the spare bedroom, where she must have seen that robbery had been committed, since an open box lay in the middle of the floor. She gave no alarm however, and it was only when Adams called out: "Where is your mistress?" that she finally went into the room of the murder. It must be admitted that this seems strange conduct, and only explicable, if it can be said to be explicable, by great want of intelligence and grasp of the situation.

On Tuesday, December 22nd, the morning after the murder, the Glasgow police circulated a description of the murderer, founded upon the joint impressions of Adams and of Lambie. It ran thus:

"A man between 25 and 30 years of age, five foot eight or nine inches in height, slim build, dark hair, clean-shaven, dressed in light grey overcoat and dark cloth cap."

Four days later, however, upon Christmas Day, the police found themselves in a position to give a more detailed description:

"The man wanted is about 28 or 30 years of age, tall and thin, with his face shaved clear of all hair, while a distinctive feature is that his nose is slightly turned to one side. The witness thinks the twist is to the right side. He wore one of the popular tweed hats known as Donegal hats, and a fawn coloured overcoat which might have been a waterproof, also dark trousers and brown boots."

The material from which these further points were gathered, came from a young girl of fifteen, in humble life, named Mary Barrowman. According to this new evidence, the witness was passing the scene of the murder shortly after seven o'clock upon the fatal night. She saw a man run hurriedly down the steps, and he passed her under a lamp-post. The incandescent light shone clearly upon him. He ran on, knocking against the witness in his haste, and disappeared round a corner. On hearing later of the murder, she connected this incident with it. Her general recollections of the man were as given in the description, and the grey coat and cloth cap of the first two witnesses were given up in favour of the fawn coat and round Donegal hat of the young girl. Since she had seen no peculiarity in his walk, and they had seen none in his nose, there is really nothing the same in the two descriptions save the "clean-shaven," the "slim build" and the approximate age.

It was on the evening of Christmas Day that the police came at last upon a definite clue. It was brought to their notice that a German Jew of the assumed name of Oscar Slater had been endeavouring to dispose of the pawn ticket of a crescent diamond brooch of about the same value as the missing one. Also, that in a general way, he bore a resemblance to the published description. Still more hopeful did this clue appear when, upon raiding the lodgings in which this man and his mistress lived, it was found that they had left Glasgow that very night by the nine o'clock train, with tickets (over this point there was some clash of evidence) either for Liverpool or London. Three days later, the Glasgow police learned that the couple had actually sailed upon December 26th upon the Lusitania for New York under the name of Mr. and Mrs. Otto Sando. It must be admitted that in all these proceedings the Glasgow police showed considerable deliberation. The original information had been given at the Central Police

Office shortly after six o'clock, and a detective was actually making enquiries at Slater's flat at seven-thirty, yet no watch was kept upon his movements, and he was allowed to leave between eight and nine, untraced and unquestioned. Even stranger was the Liverpool departure. He was known to have got away in the southbound train upon the Friday evening. A great liner sails from Liverpool upon the Saturday. One would have imagined that early on the Saturday morning steps would have been taken to block his method of escape. However, as a fact, it was not done, and as it proved it is as well for the cause of justice, since it had the effect that two judicial processes were needed, an American and a Scottish, which enables an interesting comparison to be made between the evidence of the principal witnesses.

Oscar Slater was at once arrested upon arriving at New York, and his seven trunks of baggage were impounded and sealed. On the face of it there was a good case against him, for he had undoubtedly pawned a diamond brooch, and he had subsequently fled under a false name for America. The Glasgow police had reason to think that they had got their man. Two officers, accompanied by the witnesses to identity-Adams, Lambie and Barrowman-set off at once to carry through the extradition proceedings and bring the suspect back to be tried for his offence. In the New York Court they first set eyes upon the prisoner, and each of them, in terms which will be afterwards described, expressed the opinion that he was at any rate exceedingly like the person they had seen in Glasgow. Their actual identification of him was vitiated by the fact that Adams and Barrowman had been shown his photographs before attending the Court, and also that he was led past them, an obvious prisoner, whilst they were waiting in the corridor. Still, however much one may discount the actual identification, it cannot be denied that each witness saw a close resemblance between the man before them and the man whom they had seen in Glasgow. So far at every stage the case against the accused was becoming more menacing. Any doubt as to extradition was speedily set at rest by the prisoner's announcement that he was prepared, without compulsion, to return to Scotland and to stand his trial. One may well refuse to give him any excessive credit for this surrender, since he may have been persuaded that things were going against him, but still the fact remains (and it was never, so far as I can trace, mentioned at his subsequent trial), that he gave himself up of his own free will to justice. On February 21st Oscar Slater was back in Glasgow once more, and on May 3rd his trial took place at the High Court in Edinburgh.

But already the very bottom of the case had dropped out. The starting link of what had seemed an imposing chain, had suddenly broken. It will be remembered that the original suspicion of Slater was founded upon the fact that he had pawned a crescent diamond brooch. The ticket was found upon him, and the brooch recovered. It was not the one which was missing from the room of the murdered woman, and it had belonged for years to Slater, who had repeatedly pawned it before. This was shown beyond all cavil or dispute. The case of the police might well seem desperate after this, since if Slater were indeed guilty, it would mean that by pure chance they had pursued the right man. The coincidence involved in such a supposition would seem to pass the limits of all probability.

Apart from this crushing fact, several of the other points of the prosecution had already shown themselves to be worthless. It had seemed at first that Slater's departure had been sudden and unpremeditated-the flight of a guilty man. It was quickly proved that this was not so. In the Bohemian clubs which he frequented-He was by profession a peddling jeweller and a man of disreputable, though not criminal habits. It had for weeks before the date of the crime been known that he purported to go to some business associates in America. A correspondence, which was produced, showed the arrangements which had been made, long before the crime, for his emigration, though it should be added that the actual determination of the date and taking of the ticket were subsequent to the tragedy.

This hurrying-up of the departure certainly deserves close scrutiny. According to the evidence of his mistress and of the servant, Slater had received two letters upon the morning of December 21st. Neither of these were produced at the trial. One was said to be from a Mr. Rogers, a friend of Slater's in London, telling him that Slater's wife was bothering him for money. The second was said to be from one Devoto, a former partner of Slater's asking him to join him in San Francisco. Even if the letters had been destroyed, one would imagine that these statements as to the letters could be disproved or corroborated by either the Crown or the defence. They are of considerable importance, as giving the alleged reasons why Slater hurried up a departure which had been previously announced as for January. I cannot find, however, that in the actual trial anything definite was ascertained upon the matter.

Another point had already been scored against the prosecution in that the seven trunks which contained the whole effects of the prisoner, yielded nothing of real importance. There were a felt hat and two cloth ones, but none which correspond with the Donegal of the original description. A light-coloured waterproof coat was among the outfit. If the weapon with which the deed was done was carried off in the pocket of the assassin's overcoat-and it is difficult to say how else he could have carried it, then the pocket must, one would suppose, be crusted with blood, since the crime was a most sanguinary one. No such marks were discovered, nor were the police fortunate as to the weapon. It is true that a hammer was found in the trunk, but it was clearly shown to have been purchased in one of those cheap half-crown sets of tools which are tied upon a card, was an extremely light and fragile instrument, and utterly incapable in the eyes of commonsense of inflicting those terrific injuries which had shattered the old lady's skull. It is said by the prosecution to bear some marks of having been scraped or cleaned, but this was vigorously denied by the defence, and the police do not appear to have pushed the matter to the obvious test of removing the metal work, when they must, had this been indeed the weapon, have certainly found some soakage of blood into the wood under the edges of the iron cheeks or head. But a glance at a facsimile of this puny weapon would convince an impartial person that any task beyond fixing a tin-tack, or cracking a small bit of coal, would be above its strength. It may fairly be said that before the trial had begun, the three important points of the pawned jewel, the supposed flight, and the evidence from clothing and weapon, had each either broken down completely, or become exceedingly attenuated.

Let us see now what there was upon the other side. The evidence for the prosecution really resolved itself into two sets of witnesses for identification. The first set were those who had actually seen the murderer, and included Adams, Helen Lambie, and the girl Barrowman. The second set consisted of twelve people who had, at various dates, seen a man frequenting the street in which Miss Gilchrist lived, and loitering in a suspicious manner before the house. All of these, some with confidence, but most of them with reserve, were prepared to identify the prisoner with this unknown man. What the police never could produce, however, was the essential thing, and that was the least connecting link between Slater and Miss Gilchrist, or any explanation how a foreigner in Glasgow could even know of the existence, to say nothing of the wealth, of a retired old lady, who had few acquaintances and seldom left her guarded flat.

It is notorious that nothing is more tricky than evidence of identification. In the Beck case there were, if I remember right, some ten witnesses who had seen the real criminal under normal circumstances, and yet they were all prepared to swear to the wrong man. In the case of Oscar Slater, the first three witnesses saw their man under conditions of excitement, while the second group saw the loiterer in the street under various lights, and in a fashion which was always more or less casual. It is right, therefore, that in assigning its due weight to this evidence, one should examine it with some care. We shall first take the three people who actually saw the murderer.

There seems to have been some discrepancy between them from the first, since, as has already been pointed out, the description published from the data of Adams and Lambie, was modified after Barrowman had given her information. Adams and Lambie said:

"A man between twenty-five and thirty years of age, 5 feet 8 or 9 inches in height, slim build, dark hair, clean shaven, dressed in light grey overcoat and dark cloth cap."

After collaboration with Barrowman the description became:

"Twenty-eight or thirty years of age, tall and thin, clean shaven, his nose slightly turned to one side. Wore one of the popular round tweed hats known as Donegal hats, and a fawn-coloured overcoat which might have been a waterproof, also dark trousers and brown boots."

Apart from the additions in the second description there are, it will be observed, two actual discrepancies in the shape of the hat and the colour of the coat.

As to how far either of these descriptions tallies with Slater, it may be stated here that the accused was thirty-seven years of age, that he was above the medium height, that his nose was not twisted, but was depressed at the end, as if it had at some time been broken, and finally that eight witnesses were called upon to prove that, on the date of the murder, the accused wore a short but noticeable moustache.

I have before me a verbatim stenographic report of the proceedings in New York and also in Edinburgh, furnished by the kindness of Shaughnessy & Co., solicitors, of Glasgow, who are still contending for the interests of their unfortunate client. I will here compare the terms of the identification in the two Courts: Helen Lambie, New York, January 26th, 1909.

Q. "Do you see the man here you saw there?"

A. "One is very suspicious, if anything."

Q. "Describe him."

A. "The clothes he had on that night he hasn't got on to-day —but his face I could not tell. I never saw his face."

(Having described a peculiarity of walk, she was asked):

Q. "Is that man in the room?"

A. "Yes, he is, sir."

Q. "Point him out."

A. "I would not like to say."

(After some pressure and argument she pointed to Slater, who had been led past her in the corridor between two officers, when both she and Barrowman had exclaimed: "That is the man," or "I could nearly swear that is the man.")

Q. "Didn't you say you did not see the man's face?"

A. "Neither I did. I saw the walk."

The reader must bear in mind that Lambie's only chance of seeing the man's walk was in the four steps or so down the passage. It was never at any time shown that there was any marked peculiarity about Slater's walk.

Now take Helen Lambie's identification in Edinburgh, May 9th, 1909.

Q. "How did you identify him in America?"

A. "By his walk and height, his dark hair and the side of his face."

Q. "You were not quite sure of him at first in America?"

A. "Yes, I was quite sure."

Q. "Why did you say you were only suspicions?"

A. "It was a mistake."

Q. "What did you mean in America by saying that you never saw his face if, in point of fact, you did see it so as to help you to recognise it? What did you mean?"

A. "Nothing."

On further cross-examination she declared that when she said that she had never seen the man's face she meant that she had never seen the "broad of it" but had seen it sideways.

Here it will be observed that Helen Lambie's evidence had greatly stiffened during the three months between the New York and the Edinburgh proceedings. In so aggressively positive a frame of mind was she on the later occasion, that, on being shown Slater's overcoat and asked if it resembled the murderer's, she answered twice over: "That is the coat," although it had not yet been unrolled, and though it was not light grey, which was the colour in her own original description. It should not be forgotten in dealing with the evidence of Lambie and Adams that they are utterly disagreed as to so easily fixed a thing as their own proceedings after the hall door was opened, Adams swearing that Lambie walked to nearly the end of the hall, and Lambie that she remained upon the doormat. Without deciding which was right, it is clear that the incident must shake one's confidence in one or other of them as a witness.

In the case of Adams the evidence was given with moderation, and was substantially the same in America and in Scotland.

"I couldn't say positively. This man (indicating Slater) is not at all unlike him."

Q. "Did you notice a crooked nose?"

A. "No."

Q. "Anything remarkable about his walk?"

A. "No."

Q. "You don't swear this is the man you saw?"

A. "No, sir. He resembles the man, that is all that I can say."

In reply to the same general questions in Edinburgh, he said:

"I would not like to swear he is the man. I am a little near-sighted. He resembles the man closely."

Barrowman, the girl of fifteen, had met the man presumed to be the murderer in the street, and taken one passing glance at him under a gas lamp on a wet December's night-difficult circumstances for an identification. She used these words in New York:

"That man here is something like him," which she afterwards amended to "very like him." She admitted that a picture of the man she was expected to identify had been shown to her before she came into the Court. Her one point by which she claimed to recognise the man was the crooked nose. This crooked nose was not much more apparent to others than the peculiarity of walk which so greatly impressed Helen Lambie that, after seeing half a dozen steps of it, she could identify it with confidence. In Edinburgh Barrowman, like Lambie, was very much more certain than in New York. The further they got from the event, the easier apparently did recognition become. "Yes, that is the man who knocked against me that night," she said. It is remarkable that both these females, Lambie and Barrowman, swore that though they were thrown together in this journey out to New York, and actually shared the same cabin, they never once talked of the object of their mission or compared notes as to the man they were about to identify. For girls of the respective ages of fifteen and twenty-one this certainly furnishes a unique example of self-restraint.

These, then, are the three identifications by the only people who saw the murderer. Had the diamond brooch clue been authentic, and these identifications come upon the top of it, they would undoubtedly have been strongly corroborative. But when the brooch has been shown to be a complete mistake, I really do not understand how anyone could accept such half-hearted recognitions as being enough to establish the identity and guilt of the prisoner.

There remains the so-called identification by twelve witnesses who had seen a man loitering in the street during the weeks before the crime had been committed. I have said a "so-called" identification, for the proceedings were farcical as a real test of recognition. The witnesses had seen portraits of the accused. They were well aware that he was a foreigner, and then they were asked to pick out his swarthy Jewish physiognomy from among nine Glasgow policemen to two railway officials. Naturally they did it without hesitation, since this man was more like the dark individual whom they had seen and described than the others could be.

Read their own descriptions, however, of the man they had seen, with the details of his clothing, and they will be found in many respects to differ from each other on one hand, and in many from Slater on the other. Here is a synopsis of their impressions:

Mrs. McHafiie. —"Dark. Moustached, light overcoat, not waterproof, check trousers, spats. Black bowler hat. Nose normal."

Miss M. McHaffie. —"Seen at same time and same description. Was only prepared at first to say there was some resemblance, but 'had been thinking it over, and concluded that he was the man.'"

Miss A. M. McHaffie. —"Same as before. Had heard the man speak and noticed nothing in his accent. (Prisoner has a strong German accent.)"

Madge McHaffie (belongs to the same family). —"Dark, moustached, nose normal. Check trousers, fawn overcoat and spats. Black bowler hat. 'The prisoner was fairly like the man.'"

In connection with the identification of these four witnesses it is to be observed that neither check trousers, nor spats were found in the prisoner's luggage. As the murderer was described as being dressed in dark trousers, there was no possible reason why these clothes, if Slater owned them, should have been destroyed.

Constable Brien. —"Claimed to know the prisoner by sight. Says he was the man he saw loitering. Light coat and a hat. It was a week before the crime, and he was loitering eighty yards from the scene of it. He picked him out among five constables as the man he had seen."

Constable Walker. —"Had seen the loiterer across the street, never nearer, and after dark in December. Thought at first he was someone else whom he knew. Had heard that the man he had to identify was of foreign appearance. Picked him out from a number of detectives. The man seen had a moustache."

Euphemia Cunningham. —"Very dark, sallow, heavy featured. Clean shaven. Nose normal. Dark tweed coat. Green cap with peak."

W. Campbell. —"Had been with the previous witness. Corroborated. 'There was a general resemblance between the prisoner and the man, but he could not positively identify him.'"

Alex Gillies. —"Sallow, dark haired and clean shaven. Fawn coat. Cap. 'The prisoner resembled him, but witness could not say he was the same man.'"

R. B. Bryson. —"Black coat and vest. Black bowler hat. No overcoat. Black moustache with droop. Sallow, foreign. (This witness had seen the man the night before the murder. He appeared to be looking up at Miss Gilchrist's windows.) "

A. Nairn. —"Broad shoulders, long neck. Dark hair. Motor cap. Light overcoat to knees. Never saw the man's face. 'Oh! I will not swear in fact, but I am certain he is the man I saw-but I will not swear.'"

Mrs. Liddell. —"Peculiar nose. Clear complexion, not sallow. Dark, clean shaven, brown tweed cap. Brown tweed coat with hemmed edge. Delicate man 'rather drawn together.' She believed that prisoner was the man. Saw him in the street immediately before the murder."

These are the twelve witnesses as to the identify of the mysterious stranger. In the first place there is no evidence whatever that this lounger in the street had really anything to do with the murder. It is just as probable that he had some vulgar amour, and was waiting for his girl to run out to him. What could a man who was planning murder hope to gain by standing nights beforehand eighty and a hundred yards away from the place in the darkness? But supposing that we waive this point and examine the plain question as to whether Slater was the same man as the loiterer, we find ourselves faced by a mass of difficulties and contradictions. Two of the most precise witnesses were Nairn and Bryson who saw the stranger upon the Sunday night preceding the murder. Upon that night Slater had an unshaken alibi, vouched for not only by the girl, Antoine, with whom he lived, and their servant, Schmalz, but by an acquaintance, Samuel Reid, who had been with him from six to ten-thirty. This positive evidence, which was quite unshaken in cross examination, must completely destroy the surmises of the stranger and Slater. Then come the four witnesses of the McHaffie family who are all strong upon check trousers and spats, articles of dress which were never traced to the prisoner. Finally, apart from the discrepancies about the moustache, there is a mixture of bowler hats, green caps, brown caps, and motor caps which leave a most confused and indefinite impression in the mind. Evidence of this kind might be of some value if supplementary to some strong ascertained fact, but to attempt to build upon such an identification alone is to construct the whole case upon shifting sand.

The reader has already a grasp of the facts, but some fresh details came out at the trial which may be enumerated here. They have to be lightly touched upon within the limits of such an argument as this, but those who desire a fuller summary will find it in an account of the trial published by Hodge of Edinburgh, and ably edited by William Roughead, W.S. On this book and on the verbatim precognitions and shorthand account of the American proceedings, I base my own examination of case. First, as to Slater's movements upon the day of the crime. He began the day, according to the account of himself and the women, by the receipt of the two letters already referred to, which caused him to hasten his journey to America. The whole day seems to have been occupied by preparations for his impending departure. He gave his servant Schmalz notice as from next Saturday. Before five (as was shown by the postmark upon the envelope), he wrote to a post office in London, where he had some money on deposit. At 6.12 a telegram was sent in his name and presumably by him from the Central Station to Dent, London, for his watch, which was being repaired. According to the evidence of two witnesses he was seen in a billiard room at 6.20. The murder, it will be remembered, was done at seven. He remained about ten minutes in the billiard room, and left some time between 6.30 and 6.40. Rathman, one of these witnesses, deposed that he had at the time a moustache about a quarter of an inch long, which was so noticeable that no one could take him for a clean-shaven man. Antoine, his mistress, and Schmalz, the servant, both deposed that Slater dined at home at 7 o'clock. The evidence of the girl is no doubt suspect, but there was no possible reason why the dismissed servant Schmalz should perjure herself for the sake of her ex-employer. The distance between Slater's flat and that of Miss Gilchrist is about a quarter of a mile. From the billiard room to Slater's flat is about a mile. He had to go for the hammer and bring it back, unless he had it jutting out of his pocket all day. But unless the evidence of the two women is entirely set aside, enough has been said to show that there was no time for the commission by him of such a crime and the hiding of the traces which it would leave behind it. At 9.45 that night, Slater was engaged in his usual occupation of trying to raise the wind at some small gambling club. The club-master saw no discomposure about his dress (which was the same as, according to the Crown, he had done this bloody crime in), and swore that he was then wearing a short moustache "like stubble," thus corroborating Rathman. It will be remembered that Lambie and Barrowman both swore that the murderer was clean shaven. On December 24th, three days after the murder, Slater was shown at Cook's Office, bargaining for a berth in the "Lusitania" for his so-called wife and himself. He made no secret that he was going by that ship, but gave his real name and address and declared finally that he would take his berth in Liverpool, which he did. Among other confidants as to the ship was a barber, the last person one would think to whom secrets would be confided. Certainly, if this were a flight, it is hard to say what an open departure would be. In Liverpool he took his passage under the assumed name of Otto Sando. This he did, according to his own account, because he had reason to fear pursuit from his real wife, and wished to cover his traces. This may or may not be the truth, but it is undoubtedly the fact that Slater, who was a disreputable, rolling-stone of a man, had already assumed several aliases in the course of his career. It is to be noted that there was nothing at all secret about his departure from Glasgow, and that he carried off all his luggage with him in a perfectly open manner.

The reader is now in possession of the main facts, save those which are either unessential, or redundant. It will be observed that save for the identifications, the value of which can be estimated, there is really no single point of connection between the crime and the alleged criminal. It may be argued that the existence of the hammer is such a point; but what household in the land is devoid of a hammer? It is to be remembered that if Slater committed the murder with this hammer, he must have taken it with him in order to commit the crime, since it could be no use to him in forcing an entrance. But what man in his senses, planning a deliberate murder, would take with him a weapon which was light, frail, and so long that it must project from any pocket? The nearest lump of stone upon the road would serve his purpose better than that. Again, it must in its blood-soaked condition have been in his pocket when he came away from the crime. The Crown never attempted to prove either blood-stains in a pocket, or the fact that any clothes had been burned. If Slater destroyed clothes, he would naturally have destroyed the hammer, too. Even one of the two medical witnesses of the prosecution was driven to say that he should not have expected such a weapon to cause such wounds.

It may well be that in this summary of the evidence, I may seem to have stated the case entirely from the point of view of the defence. In reply, I would only ask the reader to take the trouble to read the extended evidence. ("Trial of Oscar Slater," Hodge & Co., Edinburgh.)

If he will do so, he will realise that without a conscious mental effort towards special pleading, there is no other way in which the story can be told. The facts are on one side. The conjectures, the unsatisfactory identifications, the damaging flaws, and the very strong prejudices upon the other.

Now for the trial itself. The case was opened for the Crown by the Lord-Advocate, in a speech which faithfully represented the excited feeling of the time. It was vigorous to the point of being passionate, and its effect upon the jury was reflected in their ultimate verdict. The Lord-Advocate spoke, as I understand, without notes, a procedure which may well add to eloquence while subtracting from accuracy. It is to this fact that one must attribute a most fatal mis-statement which could not fail, coming under such circumstances from so high an authority, to make a deep impression upon his hearers. For some reason, this mis-statement does not appear to have been corrected at the moment by either the Judge or the defending counsel. It was the one really damaging allegation-so damaging that had I myself been upon the jury and believed it to be true, I should have recorded my verdict against the prisoner, and yet this one fatal point had no substance at all in fact. In this incident alone, there seems to me to lie good ground for a revision of the sentence, or a reference of the facts to some Court or Committee of Appeal. Here is the extract from the Lord-Advocate's speech to which I allude:

"At this time he had given his name to Cook's people in Glasgow as Oscar Slater. On December 25th, the day he was to go back to Cook's Office — his name and his description and all the rest of it appear in the Glasgow papers, and he sees that the last thing in the world that he ought to do, if he studies his own safety, is to go back to Cook's Office as Oscar Slater. He accordingly proceeds to pack up all his goods and effects upon the 25th. So far as we know, he never leaves the house from the time he sees the paper, until a little after six o'clock, when he goes down to the Central Station."

Here the allegation is clearly made and it is repeated later that Oscar Slater's name was in the paper, and that, subsequently to that, he fled. Such a flight would clearly be an admission of guilt. The point is of enormous even vital importance. And yet on examination of the dates, it will be found that there is absolutely no foundation for it. It was not until the evening of the 25th that even the police heard of the existence of Slater, and it was nearly a week later that his name appeared in the papers, he being already far out upon the Atlantic. What did appear upon the 25th was the description of the murderer, already quoted: "with his face shaved clean of all hair," &c., Slater at that time having a marked moustache. Why should he take such a description to himself, or why should he forbear to carry out a journey which he had already prepared for? The point goes for absolutely nothing when examined, and yet if the minds of the jury were at all befogged as to the dates, the definite assertion of the Lord-Advocate, twice repeated, that Slater's name had been published before his flight, was bound to have a most grave and prejudiced effect.

Some of the Lord-Advocate's other statements are certainly surprising. Thus he says: "The prisoner is hopelessly unable to produce a single witness who says that he was anywhere else than at the scene of the murder that night." Let us test this assertion. Here is the evidence of Schmalz, the servant, verbatim. I may repeat that this woman was under no known obligations to Slater and had just received notice from him. The evidence of the mistress that Slater dined in the flat at seven on the night of the murder I pass, but I do not understand why Schmalz's positive corroboration should be treated by the Lord-Advocate as non-existent. The prisoner might well be "hopeless" if his witnesses were to be treated so. Could anything be more positive than this?

Q. "Did he usually come home to dinner?"
A. "Yes, always. Seven o'clock was the usual hour."
Q. "Was it sometimes nearly eight?"
A. "It was my fault. Mr. Slater was in."
Q. "But owing to your fault was it about eight before it was served?"
A. "No. Mr. Slater was in after seven, and was waiting for dinner."

This seems very definite. The murder was committed about seven. The murderer may have regained the street about ten minutes or quarter past seven. It was some distance to Slater's flat. If he had done the murder he could hardly have reached it before half-past seven at the earliest. Yet Schmalz says he was in at seven, and so does Antoine. The evidence of the woman may be good or bad, but it is difficult to understand how anyone could state that the prisoner was "hopelessly unable to produce, etc." What evidence could he give, save that of everyone who lived with him?

For the rest, the Lord-Advocate had an easy task in showing that Slater was a worthless fellow, that he lived with and possibly on a woman of easy virtue, that he had several times changed his name, and that generally he was an unsatisfactory Bohemian. No actual criminal record was shown against him. Early in his speech, the Lord-Advocate remarked that he would show later how Slater may have come to know that Miss Gilchrist owned the jewels. No further reference appears to have been made to the matter, and his promise was therefore never fulfilled, though it is clearly of the utmost importance. Later, he stated that from the appearance of the wounds, they Must have been done by a small hammer. There is no "must" in the matter, for it is clear that many other weapons, a burglar's jemmy, for example, would have produced the same effect. He then makes the good point that the prisoner dealt in precious stones, and could therefore dispose of the proceeds of such a robbery. The criminal, he added, was clearly someone who had no acquaintance with the inside of the house, and did not know where the jewels were kept. "That answers to the prisoner." It also, of course, answers to practically every man in Scotland. The Lord-Advocate then gave a summary of the evidence as to the man seen by various witnesses in the street. "Gentlemen, if that was the prisoner, how do you account for his presence there?" Of course, the whole point lies in the italicised phrase. There was, it must be admitted, a consensus of opinion among the witnesses that the prisoner was the man. But what was it compared to the consensus of opinion which wrongfully condemned Beck to penal servitude? The counsel laid considerable stress upon the fact that Mrs. Liddell (one of the Adams family) had seen a man only a few minutes before the murder, loitering in the street, and identified him as Slater. The dress of the man seen in the street was very different from that given as the murderer's. He had a heavy tweed mixture coat of a brownish hue, and a brown peaked cap. The original identification by Mrs. Liddell was conveyed in the words: "One, slightly," when she was asked if any of a group at the police station resembled the man she had seen. Afterwards, like every other female witness, she became more positive. She declared that she had the clearest recollection of the man's face, and yet refused to commit herself as to whether he was shaven or moustached.

We have then the recognitions of Lambie, Adams and Barrowman, with their limitations and developments, which have been already discussed. Then comes the question of the so-called "flight" and the change of name upon the steamer. Had the prisoner been a man who had never before changed his name, this incident would be more striking. But the short glimpse we obtain of his previous life show several changes of name, and it has not been suggested that each of them was the consequence of a crime. He seems to have been in debt in Glasgow and he also appears to have had reasons for getting away from the pursuit of an ill-used wife. The Lord-Advocate said that the change of name "could not be explained consistently with innocence." That may be true enough, but the change can surely be explained on some cause less grave than murder. Finally, after showing very truly that Slater was a great liar and that not a word he said need be believed unless there were corroboration, the Lord-Advocate wound up with the words: "My submission to you is that this guilt has been brought fairly home to him, that no shadow of doubt exists, that there is no reasonable doubt that he was the perpetrator of this foul murder." The verdict showed that the jury, under the spell of the Lord-Advocate's eloquence, shared this view, but, viewing it in colder blood, it is difficult to see upon what grounds he made so confident an assertion.

Mr. M'Clure, who conducted the defence, spoke truly when, in opening his speech, he declared that "he had to fight a most unfair fight against public prejudice, roused with a fury

I do not remember to have seen in any other case." Still he fought this fight bravely and with scrupulous moderation. His appeals were all to reason and never to emotion. He showed how clearly the prisoner had expressed his intention of going to America, weeks before the murder, and how every preparation had been made. On the day after the murder he had told witnesses that he was going to America and had discussed the advantages of various lines, finally telling one of them the particular boat in which he did eventually travel, curious proceedings for a fugitive from justice. Mr. M'Clure described the movements of the prisoner on the night of the murder, after the crime had been committed, showing that he was wearing the very clothes in which the theory of the prosecution made him do the deed, as if such a deed could be done without leaving its traces. He showed incidentally (it is a small point, but a human one) that one of the last actions of Slater in Glasgow was to take great trouble to get an English five-pound note in order to send it as a Christmas present to his parents in Germany. A man who could do this was not all bad. Finally, Mr. M'Clure exposed very clearly the many discrepancies as to identification and warned the jury solemnly as to the dangers which have been so often proved to lurk in this class of evidence. Altogether, it was a broad, comprehensive reply, though where so many points were involved, it is natural that some few may have been overlooked. One does not, for example, find the counsel as insistent as one might expect upon such points as, the failure of the Crown to show how Slater could have known anything at all about the existence of Miss Gilchrist and her jewels, how he got into the flat, and what became of the brooch which, according to their theory, he had carried off. It is ungracious to suggest any additions to so earnest a defence, and no doubt one who is dependent upon printed accounts of the matter may miss points which were actually made, but not placed upon record.

Only on one point must Mr. M'Clure's judgment be questioned, and that is on the most difficult one, which a criminal counsel has ever to decide. He did not place his man in the box. This should very properly be taken as a sign of weakness. I have no means of saying what considerations led Mr. M'Clure to this determination. It certainly told against his client. In the masterly memorial for reprieve drawn up by Slater's solicitor, the late Mr. Spiers, it is stated with the full inner knowledge which that solicitor had, that Slater was all along anxious to give evidence on his own behalf. "He was advised by his counsel not to do so, but not from any knowledge of guilt. He had undergone the strain of a four days' trial. He speaks rather broken English, although quite intelligible-with a foreign accent, and he had been in custody since January." It must be admitted that these reasons are very unconvincing. It is much more probable that the counsel decided that i purely negative evidence which his client could give upon the crime would be dearly paid for by the long recital of sordid amours and blackguard experiences which would be drawn from him on cross-examination and have the most damning effect upon the minds of a respectable Edinburgh jury. And yet, perhaps, counsel did not sufficiently consider the prejudice which is excited-and rightly excited — against the prisoner who shuns the box. Some of this prejudice might have been removed if it had been made more clear that Slater had volunteered to come over and stand his trial of his own free will, without waiting for the verdict of the extradition proceedings.

There remains the summing up of Lord Guthrie. His Lordship threw out the surmise that the assassin may well have gone to the flat without any intention of murder. This is certainly possible, but in the highest degree improbable. He commented with great severity upon Slater's general character. In his summing-up of the case, he recapitulated the familiar facts in an impartial fashion, concluding with the words, "I suppose that you all think that the prisoner possibly is the murderer. You may very likely all think that he probably is the murderer. That, however, will not entitle you to convict him. The Crown have undertaken to prove that he is the murderer. That is the question you have to consider. If you think there is no reasonable doubt about it, you will convict him; if you think there is, you will acquit him."

In an hour and ten minutes the jury had made up their mind. By a majority they found the prisoner guilty. Out of fifteen, nine, as was afterwards shown, were for guilty, five for non-proven, and one for not guilty. By English law, a new trial would have been needed, ending, possibly, as in the Gardiner case, in the complete acquittal of the prisoner. By Scotch law the majority verdict held good.

"I know nothing about the affair, absolutely nothing," cried the prisoner in a frenzy of despair. "I never heard the name. I know nothing about the affair. I do not know how I could be connected with the affair. I know nothing about it. I came from America on my own account. I can say no more."

Sentence of death was then passed.

The verdict was, it is said, a complete surprise to most of those in the Court, and certainly is surprising when examined after the event. I do not see how any reasonable man can carefully weigh the evidence and not admit that when the unfortunate prisoner cried, "I know nothing about it," he was possibly, and even probably, speaking the literal truth.

Consider the monstrous coincidence which is involved in his guilt, the coincidence that the police owing to their mistake over the brooch, by pure chance started out in pursuit of the right man. Which is A Priori the more probable: That such an unheard-of million-to-one coincidence should have occurred, Or, that the police, having committed themselves to the theory that he was the murderer, refused to admit that they were wrong when the bottom fell out of the original case, and persevered in the hope that vague identifications of a queer-looking foreigner would justify their original action? Outside these identifications, I must repeat once again there is nothing to couple Slater with the murder, or to show that he ever knew, or could have known that such a person as Miss Gilchrist existed.

The admirable memorial for a reprieve drawn up by the solicitors for the defence, and re-produced at the end of this pamphlet, was signed by 20,000 members of the public, and had the effect of changing the death sentence to one of penal servitude for life. The sentence was passed on May 6th. For twenty days the man was left in doubt, and the written reprieve only arrived on May 26th within twenty-four hours of the time for the execution. On July 8th Slater was conveyed to the Peterhead Convict prison. There he has now been for three years, and there he still remains.

I cannot help in my own mind comparing the case of Oscar Slater with another, which I had occasion to examine-that of George Edalji. I must admit that they are not of the same class. George Edalji was a youth of exemplary character. Oscar Slater was a blackguard. George Edalji was physically incapable of the crime for which he suffered three years' imprisonment (years for which he has not received, after his innocence was established, one shilling of compensation from the nation). Oscar Slater might conceivably have committed the murder, but the balance of proof and probability seems entirely against it. Thus, one cannot feel the same burning sense of injustice over the matter. And yet I trust for the sake of our character not only for justice, but for intelligence, that the judgment may in some way be reconsidered and the man's present punishment allowed to atone for those irregularities of life which helped to make his conviction possible.

Before leaving the case it is interesting to see how far this curious crime may be reconstructed and whether any possible light can be thrown upon it. Using second-hand material one cannot hope to do more than indicate certain possibilities which may already have been considered and tested by the police. The trouble, however, with all police prosecutions is that, having once got what they imagine to be their man, they are not very open to any line of investigation which might lead to other conclusions. Everything which will not fit into the official theory is liable to be excluded. One might make a few isolated comments on the case which may at least give rise to some interesting trains of thought.

One question which has to be asked was whether the assassin was after the jewels at all. It might be urged that the type of man described by the spectators was by no means that of the ordinary thief. When he reached the bedroom and lit the gas, he did not at once seize the watch and rings which were lying openly exposed upon the dressing-table. He did not pick up a half- sovereign which was lying on the dining-room table. His attention was given to a wooden box, the lid of which he wrenched open. (This, I think, was "the breaking of sticks" heard by Adams.) The papers in it were strewed on the ground. Were the papers his object, and the final abstraction of one diamond brooch a mere blind ? Personally, I can only point out the possibility of such a solution. On the other hand, it might be urged, if the thief's action seems inconsequential, that Adams had rung and that he already found himself in a desperate situation. It might be said also that save a will it would be difficult to imagine any paper which would account for such an enterprise, while the jewels, on the other hand, were an obvious mark for whoever knew of their existence.

Presuming that the assassin was indeed after the jewels, it is very instructive to note his knowledge of their location, and also its limitations. Why did he go straight into the spare bedroom where the jewels were actually kept? The same question may be asked with equal force if we consider that he was after the papers. Why the spare bedroom? Any knowledge gathered from outside (by a watcher in the back-yard for example) would go to the length of ascertaining which was the old lady's room. One would expect a robber who had gained his information thus, to go straight to that chamber. But this man did not do so. He went straight to the unlikely room in which both jewels and papers actually were. Is not this remarkably suggestive? Does it not pre-suppose a previous acquaintance with the inside of the flat and the ways of its owner?

But now note the limitations of the knowledge. If it were the jewels he was after, he knew what room they were in, but not in what part of the room. A fuller knowledge would have told him they were kept in the wardrobe. And yet he searched a box. If he was after papers, his information was complete; but if he was indeed after the jewels, then we can say that he had the knowledge of one who is conversant, but not intimately conversant, with the household arrangements. To this we may add that he would seem to have shown ignorance of the habits of the inmates, or he would surely have chosen Lambie's afternoon or evening out for his attempt, and not have done it at a time when the girl was bound to be back within a very few minutes. What men had ever visited the house? The number must have been very limited. What friends? what tradesmen? what plumbers? Who brought back the jewels after they had been stored with the jewellers when the old lady went every year to the country? One is averse to throw out vague suspicions which may give pain to innocent people, and yet it is clear that there are lines of inquiry here which should be followed up, however negative the results.

How did the murderer get in if Lambie is correct in thinking that she shut the doors? I cannot get away from the conclusion that he had duplicate keys. In that case all becomes comprehensible, for the old lady-whose faculties were quite normal-would hear the lock go and would not be alarmed, thinking that Lambie had returned before her time. Thus, she would only know her danger when the murderer rushed into the room, and would hardly have time to rise, receive the first blow, and fall, as she was found, beside the chair, upon which she had been sitting. That is intelligible. But if he had not the keys, consider the difficulties. If the old lady had opened the flat door her body would have been found in the passage. Therefore, the police were driven to the hypothesis that the old lady heard the ring, opened the lower stair door from above (as can be done in all Scotch flats) , opened the flat door, never looked over the lighted stair to see who was coming up, but returned to her chair and her magazine, leaving the door open, and a free entrance to the murderer. This is possible, but is it not in the highest degree improbable? Miss Gilchrist was nervous of robbery and would not neglect obvious precautions. The ring came immediately after the maid's departure. She could hardly have thought that it was her returning, the less so as the girl had the keys and would not need to ring. If she went as far as the hall door to open it, she only had to take another step to see who was ascending the stair. Would she not have taken it if it were only to say: "What, have you forgotten your keys?" That a nervous old lady should throw open both doors, never look to see who her visitor was, and return to her dining-room is very hard to believe.

And look at it from the murderer's point of view. He had planned out his proceedings. It is notorious that it is the easiest thing in the world to open the lower door of a Scotch flat. The blade of any penknife will do that. If he was to depend upon ringing to get at his victim, it was evidently better for him to ring at the upper door, as otherwise the chance would seem very great that she would look down, see him coming up the stair, and shut herself in. On the other hand, if he were at the upper door and she answered it, he had only to push his way in. Therefore, the latter would be his course if he rang at all. And yet the police theory is that though he rang, he rang from below. It is not what he would do, and if he did do it, it would be most unlikely that he would get in. How could he suppose that the old lady would do so incredible a thing as leave her door open and return to her reading? If she waited, she might even up to the last instant have shut the door in his face. If one weighs all these reasons, one can hardly fail, I think, to come to the conclusion that the murderer had keys, and that the old lady never rose from her chair until the last instant, because, hearing the keys in the door, she took it for granted that the maid had come back. But if he had keys, how did he get the mould, and how did he get them made? There is a line of inquiry there. The only conceivable alternatives are, that the murderer was actually concealed in the flat when Lambie came out, and of that there is no evidence whatever, or that the visitor was some one whom the old lady knew, in which case he would naturally have been admitted.

There are still one or two singular points which invite comment. One of these, which I have incidentally mentioned, is that neither the match, the match-box, nor the box opened in the bedroom showed any marks of blood.

Yet the crime had been an extraordinarily bloody one. This is certainly very singular. An explanation given by Dr. Adams who was the first medical man to view the body is worthy of attention. He considered that the wounds might have been inflicted by prods downwards from the leg of a chair, in which case the seat of the chair would preserve the clothes and to some extent the hands of the murderer from bloodstains. The condition of one of the chairs seemed to him to favour this supposition. The explanation is ingenious, but I must confess that I cannot understand how such wounds could be inflicted by such an instrument. There were in particular a number of spindle-shaped cuts with a bridge of skin between them which are very suggestive. My first choice as to the weapon which inflicted these would be a burglar's jemmy, which is bifurcated at one end, while the blow which pushed the poor woman's eye into her brain would represent a thrust from the other end. Failing a jemmy, I should choose a hammer, but a very different one from the toy thing from a half-crown card of tools which was exhibited in Court. Surely commonsense would say that such an instrument could burst an eye-ball, but could not possibly drive it deep into the brain, since the short head could not penetrate nearly so far. The hammer, which I would reconstruct from the injuries would be what they call, I believe, a plasterer's ham.mer, short in the handle, long and strong in the head, with a broad fork behind. But how such a weapon could be used without the user bearing marks of it, is more than I can say. It has never been explained why a rug was laid over the murdered woman. The murderer, as his conduct before Lambie and Adams showed, was a perfectly cool person. It is at least possible that he used the rug as a shield between him and his victim while he battered her with his weapon. His clothes, if not his hands, would in this way be preserved.

I have said that it is of the first importance to trace who knew of the existence of the jewels, since this might greatly help the solution of the problem. In connection with this there is a passage in Lambie's evidence in New York which is of some importance. I give it from the stenographer's report, condensing in places:

Q. "Do you know in Glasgow a man named?"

A. "Yes, sir."

Q. "What is his business?"

A. "A book-maker."

Q. "When did you first meet him?"

A. "At a dance."

Q. "What sort of dance?"

A. "A New Year's dance." (That would be New Year of 1908.)

Q. "When did you meet him after that?"

A. "In the beginning of June."

Q. "Where?"

A. "In Glasgow."

Q. "At a street corner?"

A. "No, he came up to the house at Prince's Street."

Q. "Miss Gilchrist's house?"

A. "Yes, sir."

Q. "That was the first time since the dance?"

A. "Yes, sir."

Q. "Do you deny that you had a meeting with him by a letter received from him at a corner of a street in Glasgow?"

A. "I got a letter."

Q. "To meet him at a street corner?"

A. "Yes."

Q. "The first meeting after the dance?"

A. "Yes."

Q. "And you met him there?"

A. "Yes."

Q. "And you went out with him?"

A. "No, I did not go out with him."

Q. "You went somewhere with him, didn't you?"

A. "Yes, I made an appointment for Sunday."

Q. "Did you know anything about the man?"

A. "Yes, I did, sir."

Q. "What did you know about him?"

A. "I didn't know much."

Q. "How many times did he visit you at Miss Gilchrist's house?"

A. "Once."

Q. "Quite sure of that?"

A. "Quite sure."

Q. "Didn't he come and take tea with you there in her apartment?"

A. "That was at the Coast."

Q. "Then he came to see you at Miss Gilchrist's summer place?"

A. "Yes."

Q. "How many times?"

A. "Once."

Q. "Did he meet Miss Gilchrist then?"

A. "Yes, sir."

Q. "You introduced him?"

A. "Yes, sir."

Q. "Did she wear this diamond brooch?"

A. "I don't remember."

Q. "When did you next see him?"

A. "The first week in September."

Q. "In Glasgow?"

A. "Yes, sir."

Q. "By appointment?"

A. "Yes."

Q. "When next?"

A. "I have not met him since."

Q. "And you say he only called once at the country place?"

A. "Once, sir."

Q. "In your Glasgow deposition you say: 'He visited me at Girvan and was entertained at tea with me on Saturday night, and at dinner on Sunday with Miss Gilchrist and me.'"

A. "Yes, sir."

Q. "Then you did see him more than once in the country."

A. "Once."

He read the extract again as above.

Q. "Was that true?"

A. "Yes."

Q. "Then you invited this man to tea at Miss Gilchrist's summer house?"

A. "Yes."

Q. "On Saturday night?"

A. "Yes."

Q. "And on Sunday night?"

A. "He wasn't there."

Q. "On Sunday you invited him there to dinner with Miss Gilchrist and yourself, didn't you?"

A. "Yes, sir. I didn't invite him."

Q. "Who invited him."

A. "Miss Gilchrist."

Q. "Had you introduced him?"

A. "Yes, sir."

Q. "He was your friend, wasn't he?"

A. "Yes, sir."

Q. "She knew nothing about him?"

A. "No."

Q. "She took him to the house on your recommendation?"

A. "Yes."

Q. "Did she wear her diamonds at thisi dinner party?"

A. "I don't remember."

Q. "You told him that she was a rich woman?"

A. "Yes."

Q. "Did you tell him that she had a great many jewels?"

A. "Yes."

Q. "Have your suspicions ever turned towards this man?"

A. "Never."

Q. "Do you know of any other man who would be as familiar with those premises, the wealth of the old lady, her jewelry, and the way to get into the premises as that man?"

A. "No, sir."

Q. "Was the man you met in the hallway this man?"

A. "No, sir."

This is a condensation of a very interesting and searching piece of the cross-examination which reveals several things. One is Lambie's qualities as a witness. Another is the very curious picture of the old lady, the bookmaker and the servant-maid all sitting at dinner together. The last and most important is the fact, that a knowledge of the jewels had got out. Against the man himself there is no possible allegation. The matter was looked into by the police, and their conclusions were absolute, and were shared by those responsible for the defence. But is it to be believed that during the months which elapsed between this man acquiring this curious knowledge, and the actual crime, never once chanced to repeat to any friend, who in turn repeated it to another, the strange story of the lonely old woman and her hoard? This he would do in full innocence. It was a most natural thing to do. But, for almost the first time in the case we seem to catch some glimpse of the relation between possible cause and effect, some connection between the dead woman on one side, and outsiders on the other who had the means of knowing something of her remarkable situation.

There is just one other piece of Lambie's cross-examination, this time from the Edinburgh trial, which I would desire to quote. It did not appear in America, just as the American extract already given did not appear in Edinburgh. For the first time they come out together:

Q. "Did Miss Gilchrist use to have a dog?"

A. "Yes, an Irish terrier."

Q. "What happened to it?"

A. "It got poisoned."

Q. "When was it poisoned?"

A. "I think on the 7th or 8th of September."

Q. "Was that thought to be done by some one?"

A. "I did not think it, for I thought it might have eaten something, but Miss Gilchrist thought it was poisoned by some one."

Q. "To kill the watch-dog —was that the idea?"

A. "She did not say."

The reader should be reminded that Slater did not arrive in Glasgow until the end of October of that year. His previous residences in the town were as far back as 1901 and 1905. If the dog were indeed poisoned in anticipation of the crime, he, at least, could have had nothing to do with it.

There is one other piece of evidence which may, or may not have been of importance. It is that of Miss Brown, the schoolmistress. This lady was in court, but seems to have been called by neither side for the reason that her evidence was helpful to neither the prosecution nor the defence. She deposed that on the night of the murder, about ten minutes past seven, she saw two men running away from the scene. One of these men closely corresponded to the original description of the murderer before it was modified by Barrowman. This one was of medium build, dark hair and clean shaven, with three-quarter length grey overcoat, dark tweed cap, and both hands in his pockets. Here we have the actual assassin described to the life, and had Miss Brown declared that this man was the prisoner, she would have been a formidable addition to the witnesses for prosecution. Miss Brown, however identified Oscar Slater (after the usual absurd fashion of such identifications) as the second man, whom she describes, as of "Dark glossy hair, navy blue overcoat with velvet collar, dark trousers, black boots, something in his hand which seemed clumsier than a walking stick." One would imagine that this object in his hand would naturally be his hat, since she describes the man as bare-headed. All that can be said of this incident is that if the second man was Slater, then he certainly was not the actual murderer whose dress corresponds closely to the first, and in no particular to the second. To the Northern eye, all swarthy foreigners bear a resemblance, and that there was a swarthy man, whether foreign or not, concerned in this affair would seem to be beyond question. That there should have been two confederates, one of whom had planned the crime while the other carried it out, is a perfectly feasible supposition. Miss Brown's story does not necessarily contradict that of Barrowman, as one would imagine that the second man would join the murderer at some little distance from the scene of the crime. However, as there was no cross-examination upon the story, it is difficult to know what weight to attach to it.

Let me say in conclusion that I have had no desire in anything said in this argument, to hurt the feelings or usurp the functions of anyone, whether of the police or the criminal court, who had to do with the case. It is difficult to discuss matters from a detached point of view without giving offence. I am well aware that it is easier to theorise at a distance than to work a case out in practice whether as detective or as counsel. I leave the matter now with the hope that, even after many days, some sudden flash may be sent which will throw a light upon as brutal and callous a crime as has ever been recorded in those black annals in which the criminologist finds the materials for his study. Meanwhile it is on the conscience of the authorities, and in the last resort on that of the community that this verdict obtained under the circumstances which I have indicated, shall now be reconsidered.

Arthur Conan Doyle, Windlesham, Crowborough.

9 788027 337347